CONTENTS

Dimensions of Mass Involvement in Botswana Politics: A Test of Alternative Theories

JOHN D. HOLM
Cleveland State University

ABSTRACT

This paper is an exploration of the dimensionality of mass political involvement and the socio-economic basis of such involvement in Botswana, a developing African state. Two alternative sets of hypotheses related to this subject are considered: (1) that change in the political thought and behavior of the public is by a mobilization process; (2) that change at this level of politics fits a syncretistic model. The analysis is based on citizen reactions to the replacement of a chieftaincy system of local government by elected local councils.

With respect to political involvement itself, mobilization and syncretism are manifested in different dimensions, and the extent of each effect tends to vary with the criteria used in the derivation of the dimensions. The impact of socio-economic factors on changes in citizen political involvement also reflects both mobilization and syncretism, depending on the form of involvement being examined and the environment in which it occurs. The general conclusion of this analysis is that

AUTHOR'S NOTE: *The field research for this paper was funded by a summer research grant from Cleveland State University. A preliminary report on the data examined herein was presented at the annual meeting of the African Studies Association, Denver Colorado, November, 1971. The author is indebted to the following for their critical comments on various versions of this paper: Michael Armer, Richard Hofstetter, Leon Hurwitz, Charles Nixon, Kenneth Prewitt, Rudolph Rummel, James Schuerger, Jack Vincent, Lawrence Waters, Richard Vengroff, Richard Weisfelder, and especially Robert Charlick. The author is also very appreciative of the long hours many politicians, government officials, newspapermen and academics in Botswana have spent discussing the realities of their society and its politics. Without their kindness and patience, this project would not have been possible. Particular mention should be made in this regard of Ma Gabaake, Victor Ntsekhe, Mike Pitso, Ian Smith, and Thomas Tlou.*

*more complex theories of citizen involvement are required. The
evidence from Botswana is that mobilization processes are most substantial in passive dimensions of involvement and syncretism appears
most likely in the very intense forms of participation. Between these
polar extremes both models of explanation tend to have some
relevance; however, their usefulness is much less than at the extremes.*

INTRODUCTION

The study of political development concerns processes by which particular changes are brought about in political systems. For the most
part, analysts of this subject have concentrated on the emergence of
democratic procedures for the selection of chief policy makers, the
growth of a participant type of citizenry, and various forms of institu-
tion-building related to the emergence of the modern bureaucratic
nation-state. Scholars studying African politics have focused on this
third form of development with particular attention being paid to the
role of elites in shaping the contours of the new institutions. In the
process, much of this research has delineated the minimal extent to
which the democratic procedures are operative for the selection of chief
policy makers. Very little inquiry, however, has dealt with the character
of citizen involvement in the political institutions which are being
created, particularly at the local level where African elites often claim
popular influence is the most extensive.[1] This paper explores some of
the problems involved in the study of citizen participation in a
developing African state and suggests some tentative outlines of a
theory regarding the growth of citizen involvement.

The empirical basis for analysis is the citizen response to local
councils created in 1965 in Botswana[2] to replace a system which had
been controlled by traditional authorities and supported by colonial
civil servants. In this new context, competitive party politics have
become a reality in many council districts even though the Botswana
Democratic Party (BDP) has won overwhelmingly in both the 1966 and
1969 elections.[3] Indeed, minority parties have garnered a majority of
the seats in several councils and moved close to additional victories in a
number of others.[4] The emergence of elected councils and a political
party system has not by any means spelled the end of the Tswana chieftaincy. Not only do the tribal authorities still retain a few of their traditional functions, e.g., adjudication of petty disputes, but they also have
become involved in party politics as a real or potential opposition to the
BDP.

I. MODERNITY AND TRADITION: TWO MODELS OF CHANGE

Much of the discussion of political development in Africa is concerned with the relationship between traditional and modern authority. The former type is associated with not only chiefs, but also elders, diviners, and healers who are legitimatized on the basis of customary norms. The modern elites are those who have been extensively exposed to Western inspired socio-economic change, including a Western form of education, Christianity, mass media, nonagricultural labor, travel, and urban residence, and who claim the right to rule on the basis of constitutional norms and/or their ability to provide leadership in achieving social and economic modernization.[5] During the period shortly before and after independence, scholars placed much emphasis on the *clash* between these two elites. For instance, Wallerstein (1961: 163) writes "The effective choice [in Africa] . . . is between a one-party . . . system, which allows for some real popular participation in, and control over, the government, or anarchy, which means that power reverts to local princelings and patrons, remote from the intellectual contact and stimulation which infuses the modernizing elite of the national structures." In this model of political development, the essential stimulus for conflict is the socio-economic change which the modernizers and their supporters experience while the traditional elites, to a certain extent, and their followers remain relatively unaffected. The central hypotheses of this model for citizen politics, though often unarticulated, are:[6]

Hypothesis I — Citizen involvement in the new modern political structures is associated with withdrawal from traditional political activity by the citizen; i.e., the hypothesis of political mobilization.

Hypothesis II — Citizens who have experienced specific forms of socio-economic modernization are more likely than those who have not experienced such modernization to become involved in modern political structures, i.e., the hypothesis of socio-economic mobilization.

Both of these hypotheses usually presume a cumulative effect. One type of modern political involvement, e.g., a moral commitment to elections for selecting public officials, brings other changes, such as formation of opinion on public policy issues and participation in political party activities. And, one form of socio-economic change triggers a series of others; thus, increases in education are connected with more involvement in mass media. From this perspective, it is generally presumed that the more cumulative the political mobilization of a person, the more intensive will be the rejection of the traditional system as an arena of political involvement. Also, the presumption is that the more extensive the socio-economic change the individual experiences, the more likely he is to move toward the modern political system.[7]

Mobilization theorists do not postulate a unilinear relation between socio-economic change and increased citizen involvement in the political structures. A number stress that the impact of the social and economic changes is determined by the stage of development which has been achieved. Thus, Lerner (1958: 54-65) specifies three stages of change, i.e., urbanization, expansion of literacy, and mass media participation, which come before and provide the basis for the expansion of mass participation in the electoral system. In addition, modernization theorists conceive of the emergence of the modern polity as proceeding at different rates within particular institutional sectors. Deutsch (1961: 497-502), for instance, suggests the need to explore such realms of political change as citizen participation, national loyalty and consolidation of states. Finally, mobilization theorists often stipulate that the connection of socio-economic and political change may be substantially altered by the intervention of factors not included in the simplified form of the model. Lerner (1958: 66) asserts that in countries of low population density, which would presumably involve most African states including Botswana, literacy will not be affected by urbanization but rather respond to rises in per capita national income.

Each of these basic forms of modification of the processes postulated in hypotheses I and II will be explored in the analysis which follows. We will be concerned with both those which have been articulated heretofore and others which are suggested by the data.

The attraction and weakness of this social mobilization school is its primary concern with processes which operate independently of the specific cultural contexts of traditional societies. It is simply presumed that the populace is leaving major complexes of old commitments that are personalized, affective, and ascriptive, among other things, for a new social structure which is impersonal, bureaucratic, achievement oriented and the like. Little attention is given to the persistence of the traditional political structures or the extent to which there is a blending of traditional and modern modes of political behavior.

In reaction to this analysis, a syncretistic approach to political development has emerged in many recent studies of Africa.[8] It is argued that the "new" political structures must be studied within a conceptual framework which accounts for the interaction of modernizing influences and those emanating from the existing culture. Zolberg (1966: 128-134) suggests that two systems for the allocation of values may be present in African politics, one the traditional and the other modern. With regard to Tanzania, Miller (1966: 185) writes that a syncretistic type of traditional leader has emerged based "on the very real need of both peasants and government to have a rural intermediary." Some contend that modernizers are in no way assured of controlling traditional leaders. Indeed, analysts such as Whitaker (1970) have argued that at least at the subnational level a stable synthesis may involve the traditional authorities dominating the new government structures established both before and after independence.
[9] Underlying these various syncretistic models of political development are two general hypotheses with respect to the changing character of citizen involvement in politics:

Hypothesis III—A citizen will tend to undertake similar types of political activity in both the traditional and modern political systems; the hypothesis of political syncretism.

Hypothesis IV—Traditional and modern socio-economic variables are associated with citizen involvement in both the traditional and modern political structures; the hypothesis of socio-economic syncretism.

A crucial difference should be noted between the hypotheses of political and socio-economic syncretism as they are used in the study of political development. Discussion of political syncretism by definition must refer to a solitary person joining the old and the new in terms of perception or action. Socio-economic syncretism may occur, however, at either the individual or group level. Sometimes, it is suggested that the individual integrates both types of socio-economic factors when undertaking a particular form of political involvement. In other cases, it is argued that certain groups are affected by the traditional and others by the modern socio-economic influences but still come to the same perception or behavior.
This paper will explore the utility of the above four hypotheses for

explaining change in the character of selected dimensions of citizen involvement in Botswana local politics subsequent to the introduction of the council system in 1965. The fundamental thesis developed is that the extent of political mobilization and syncretism varies with the criteria used to identify covariation of political involvement and that the extent of socio-economic mobilization and syncretism depends on the dimension of political involvement being examined. It is propounded that mobilization patterns are manifest in more passive forms of political involvement and that syncretism is more apparent in more active realms of involvement. It is also asserted that the extent of mobilization and syncretism appears highly dependent on the historical context and socio-economic structure in which political change occurs.

The discussion is divided into five sections. The first explores the literature of political involvement as it relates to dimensions of citizen change. The second briefly delineates the general character of the sample on which the analysis is based. The third section specifies some general aspects of the historical and cultural context of Botswana politics which are relevant to the study. The fourth considers the extent to which the political mobilization and syncretism hypotheses (nos. I and III) are substantiated by the political involvement of respondents being examined. The fifth section treats the relationship between the dimensions of political involvement, discussed in the previous section, and the socio-economic structure, i.e., the hypotheses of socio-economic mobilization and syncretism (nos. II and IV).

II. INVOLVEMENT DIMENSIONS

Most studies of political involvement assume for purposes of empirical analysis that various forms of change may be subsumed under one general dimension of behavior. For instance, both Lerner (1958: 57) and Needler (1968: 863) use voter turnout as their basic index of mass participation in the modern political system. Others, such as Inkeles (1969: 1124-1131) and Nie, Powell and Prewitt (1969: 375-377), seek to be more comprehensive by combining several types of political involvement into an overall index of participant citizenship. It is very possible, however, that a number of distinct dimensions of mass participation in the political system may exist, and change in one realm will take place without any transformation occurring in another. Recently, Verba et al. (1971, 1973) employed factor analysis to demonstrate that, in six democratic countries at various stages of economic and political development, at least four dimensions of mass participant behavior could be identified: campaigning, voting, communal acts, and personalized contact with public officials. Even in Yugoslavia, the one-party system only eliminated the campaign dimension. Particularly relevant in this connection is their finding that the voting dimension has a very low correlation with the other domains of mass political action. A study of the relation of various socio-economic changes to voting, thus, may not tell us very much about the impact of these changes on other forms of modern political activity or the extent to which traditional involvement has been altered. Likewise, an index which is a composite of changes in a number of dimensions of mass political activity may not reveal much about the process of transformation in a single dimension, such as voting, or in dimensions not included in the index.[10]

In constructing the questionnaire used in this study, it was postulated that at least five dimensions of citizen political involvement [11] might exist in Botswana local politics:

(1) awareness of the legal change in local government structure from a chieftaincy to council system;

(2) moral evaluation of the change;

(3) participation in the council institutions;

(4) participation in traditional political institutions; and

(5) feelings of local political community.

Exhibit A contains a shortened version of all the items employed in each of these categories. Each question was designed to probe subjects to which the average citizen was likely to have a reaction or which concerned behavior that was at least possible for most of the populace.

The five categories of questions were developed on the basis of a number of considerations. First, it seemed very possible that awareness of the change in local government institutions would not be correlated with moral support for this change. Very simply, many citizens might oppose the transfer of power. Thus, two dimensions ought to be evident simply in terms of respondent perceptions. Second, perception of and moral support for the new structures might not be highly associated with behavioral change. A person could support the council system but have no motivation to participate. Or, he could be aware but decide to show his opposition by boycotting the elections. As a consequence, it was necessary to probe actual participation. Third, participation in the modern institutions could not be presumed to be reflective of withdrawal from the traditional system; otherwise, it would be impossible to test the extent of syncretism. Therefore, both modern and traditional forms of participation needed to be probed. Fourth, traditional participation is often postulated to be based on a sense of community. [12] For this reason, it was necessary to ask questions exploring aspects of traditional solidarity so that it would be possible to determine if this solidarity was connected with traditional participation.

While most of the questions related solely to local political considerations, several have national political significance. The study design was to include in each of the groupings of items related to modern politics at least one item which would permit some inquiry into whether the dimension postulated was strictly local in character or reflected a similar type of association with national politics. This was the rationale

EXHIBIT A

TWENTY-FOUR ORIGINAL POLITICAL INVOLVEMENT ITEMS

Items Included	Possible Responses
Extra-Local Political Information	
1. Who are the persons holding the following positions? a) MP in your area b) President of Zambia c) Leader of one of the opposition parties d) President of Botswana e) Prime Minister of South Africa	One point given for each correct answer
Legal Awareness	
2. Who decides on the building of new primary schools, the chief or the local council?	Chief or Uncertain/Council
3. Does the money collected in taxes belong to the chief or the council?	Chief or Uncertain/Council
4. Who decides where boreholes are to be sunk, the chief or the council?	Chief or Uncertain/Council
5. To whom do stray cattle belong, the chief or the council?	Chief or Uncertain/Council
6. Who has more power, the chief or the President?	Chief or Uncertain/President
Moral Support	
7. Who can allocate land better, the chief or the land boards newly established by Parliament?	Chief or Uncertain/Land Boards
8. Who is more concerned about the people, the chief or the local MP?*	Chief or Uncertain/MP
9. Who is more concerned with the people, the headman or the local councilor?	Headman or Uncertain/Local Councilor
10. Who can best unite the people in this area, the chief or the council?	Chief or Uncertain/Council
Traditional Participation	
11. Do you think it is right for villagers to go on with a project, say the building of a school, even if the chief is against the project?	No/Yes

EXHIBIT A (cont.)

Items Included	Possible Responses
12. If the chief asks you to be one of his regular advisors, would you be willing to do so?**	No/Yes
13. If the chief sends out your age-regiment, would you go with them if you had time?	No/Yes
14. When the chief summons a meeting, do you go?**	No/Yes
15. Have you ever contacted a chief or a headman to try to persuade him to make a certain decision or to change one he has already made?**	No/Yes

Council Participation

16. Have you ever become concerned about issues before your local council?	No/Yes
17. Have you ever contacted a councilor to make your opinion known on one of the council's decisions or offered a suggestion to the councilor as to what he should do?	No/Yes
18. Did you vote in the last election?	No/Yes
19. Do you belong to a political party?	No/Yes
20. Have you ever attended meetings held by the political parties?	No/Yes

Political Community

21. Have you ever thought of leaving this community and moving somewhere else?@	No/Yes
22. Do you think it would be better for your children to raise their children in another community instead of staying here?@	No/Yes
23. Do you think that people who come here from other villages outside of this tribal area should have an equal say with you in village affairs?	No/Yes
24. Do you think that you can have a say in the decisions that are made for this village as a whole?	No/Yes

---

*The MP was used because he is a very influential politician in most districts both in terms of the council itself and inducing the national government to assist local projects.

**These questions were adapted for women to make them relevant to their status within the traditional political system.

@These questions probe aspects of political community in that traditionally the family was an important component in the government structure. This is reflected for instance in the tradition that elder males speak for the entire family at political meetings.

for the inclusion of the question on extra-local political information (no. 1) and the comparison of the chief's performance with that of the member of parliament (no. 8). Also, the local elections are held at the same time as national elections; thus, voting and attending political rallies have local and extra-local meaning.

III. THE SAMPLE

Several general characteristics of the sample should be noted. It consists of 1,110 respondents who are 20 years or older and live in the 5 southern Tswana tribal areas of Tlokweng, Bamalete, Kweneng, Ngwaketse, and Kgatleng or the 2 southern towns of Gaberone and Lobatsi. Sample locations were selected within these regions by a probability method, and respondents were quota sampled within the selected areas. In the towns, streets were chosen on a random basis, and in the tribal areas, wards were identified by a similar means. The interviewers then went to a street or ward and interviewed 10 respondents, taking one from every third household. The selection of wards in the tribal areas was controlled to insure that a number of royal wards were included. In order to sample a broad spectrum of the populace, quotas were established with respect to age, sex, and economic status. All interviews were conducted in 1970 during August and the first week in September. Appendix I provides a brief evaluation of the quality of the sample.

IV. THE BOTSWANA CONTEXT

The character of the Botswana reaction to the new local government structure which the national elite created will have little meaning without some understanding of the government which has heretofore existed at the local level and the extent of change which has been thus far achieved. This section therefore presents a brief description of the nature of traditional Tswana politics, its transformation under colonial rule, and the structure and the role of the new councils.

Before the British arrived almost all the Botswana was divided among eight major political units or tribes. Each had its own chief. No permanent cooperation existed among these tribes or their rulers except when political expediency warranted or kinship bonds imposed a special obligation between two office holders. The structure of authority within the tribes is generally reputed to have been very autocratic. By custom the chief was only obligated to consult with his close relatives and subordinate headmen on most political issues. He listened to a general assembly of adult males on extremely important decisions, like war, peace and moving to a new geographic area. In practice, a chief could have his own way as long as a majority of his relatives and headmen were not strongly opposed to his ideas. When they did oppose him in substantial numbers, as Schapera (1970: 78) notes, he had to "abide by their verdict, unless he . . . [was] looking for trouble." The will of the headmen to resist a chief was limited by the fact that they had no more authority than the chief chose to grant them. The chief could reduce the territory of their rule, subordinate one headman to another, or in rare instances, depose a headman. Selection of a new headman or chief was automatic. The position went to the eldest son of the senior wife of the the former office holder. Should a particular chief become intolerably autocratic and if his advisors were unable to induce him to mend his ways, one of two options was exercised: mass migration to another tribe or murder of the chief.

With advent of the British Protectorate in 1885, the Tswana chiefs became the "primary executive authority" in local government, and the colonial officers at the local level confined themselves to the role of "giving advice and guidance." (Sillery, 1952: 211) Indeed, the British were so lax in exercising their authority over the chiefs that it was not until the middle thirties that the Protectorate Government first issued any significant regulations governing the duties of the chiefs. Even then these regulations were effectively resisted by some of the chiefs and had to be substantially modified before they could be implemented. It is generally accepted that under colonial rule the chiefs were even more autocratic and self-serving than they had been previously. They knew that their tenure depended solely on British goodwill and that the people or the headmen could do little to frustrate the exercise of chiefly prerogatives. The British for their part rarely removed a chief for mal-administration. It was not until the elected councils were established in 1966, the year of independence, that the Botswana people regained any formal control over the exercise of political authority in their local areas.

One very important base of the authority of Tswana chiefs was the traditional religion. Serving as the principal link between the people and the world of ancestors and other spirits, the chiefs were much feared and respected. When the Christian missionaries came into Botswana, most chiefs rather quickly moved to ally themselves with a particular denomination. In a number of cases, the chiefs became fervent supporters of Christianity. They not only urged conversion but also revised traditional law in conformity with Christianity. Thus, while the Church had undermined one of the sources of chieftainship authority, the substantial communal acceptance of the new religion under the leadership of the chiefs has meant that Tswana traditional authorities have very rarely been opposed by the Christian community, as has occurred in other African societies.

The only other major area of change which the chiefs facilitated was the building of primary schools in their areas. With the exception of Bathoen II of the Ngwaketse, none gave any substantial encouragement to or participated in progressive farming.[13] They rarely invested their money in a commercial enterprise. The economic improvements they undertook as local government leaders, such as waterhole management and road building, were mostly as a result of the pressure from the colonial government. The staffs they developed to carry out the expanded chiefly functions were generally of very poor quality. Finally, outside of harmonizing tribal laws with certain Christian principles, they did little to reform the traditional laws and customs to cope with an emerging market economy based on the sale of cattle and migratory labor. In effect, the chiefs moved as slowly as possible to keep up with changes arising in other parts of the community. In some instances, particularly in Bamalete, the chiefs acted as adamant defenders of tradition.

The Tswana chiefs have always played a prominent role as the symbol of tribal unity. They are properly addressed as the personification of the tribal name or the tribal totem. According to custom, both the people and their headmen cannot come together without the chief's consent. The tribe cannot make a decision except through the chief's voice. As might be expected, this close identification between the chief and the unity of the tribe affects the chief's role in modern party politics. On one hand, when the chief supports a party, it tends to have almost instant popularity in his area. For instance, the Bakgatla support the Botswana People's Party in part because the sister of the present chief campaigned publicly for it immediately before the first election. On the other hand, the chief's entry into partisan politics is viewed as uncomplimentary to his position as the unifier of his people. He is a healer of divisions and not a creator of faction. Therefore, his reputation tends to suffer even among many of his fervent supporters when he attaches himself to a party. Only in the absence of a substantial opposition party can a chief both support a party and maintain his traditional popular prestige.

African self-government was achieved at the national level in Botswana in 1965. One of the first actions of the new legislature dominated by Seretse Khama and his BDP was to pass a law creating elected local councils in both towns and rural areas. Within three years, these councils obtained most of the powers the chiefs had formerly exercised. Most significantly, all decisions relating to land and water distribution—very important questions in an arid climate—were made by the local council and its committees. The council also was to allocate funds for primary education in the district—an issue of highly explosive nature in almost all African polities. Other functions the councils have acquired are development and administration of health and sanitation services, issuance of permits for commercial undertakings and housing construction, promotion of secondary road construction, and supervision of the collection of stray cattle and their return to their owners. A veritable revolution has occurred in formal authority. The only major powers the chiefs retain are the administration of courts for petty offenses and the right to call public meetings. While almost every council has elected the chief as its chairman, the civil servants respond to the orders of the chairmen of the various council committees. The chief is generally a figure-head leader of the council except in those instances where he carries influence with committee chairmen. In effect, he lends the council his prestige while the councilors attempt to persuade the people that they are better rulers than he.

The chiefs have fought this transformation, but they have for the most part been unsuccessful in bringing the councils under their control. In Ngwaketse, Bathoen II, who had been chief for over forty years, actually resigned in 1969 to head a slate of candidates supportive of the chieftaincy. The Government has employed several means to counter the subversion of the councils by the traditional authorities. Most importantly, it has the right to appoint councilors in addition to those elected by the people. In part, it has used this power to insure that a majority of the councilors will not be inclined to submit to the will of the local chief. Second, the Ministry of Local Government has in various ways pressured the chiefs and headmen to minimize their intervention in local elections. It has not been completely successful, but almost all political activity by traditional authorities has been kept to a covert level at election time, thus reducing their impact. Third, as chairmen of their councils, the chiefs have been somewhat muzzled in public. They must speak about council matters as its representative rather than as an opponent of the new structure. Finally, the Government party, the BDP, has many in its leadership ranks who are of high traditional status but have, for one reason or another, rejected positions in the tribal structure and chosen rather to seek their political fortune in electoral politics. Having considerable traditional prestige with the people as a whole, the BDP does not feel any great compulsion to compromise with the chiefs by giving them substantial influence in the operation of the local councils.

V. DIMENSIONS OF POLITICAL INVOLVEMENT IN BOTSWANA

The objective of this section is to explore the dimensionality of mass involvement in the traditional and councilmatic political structures which have just been described. The data being examined are responses to the twenty-four political involvement items in Exhibit A which were postulated to identify five aspects of local politics. Our analysis in this section will concern the extent to which these items confirm Hypothesis I, i.e., that contact with the modern system is inversely related to contacts with the traditional system (political mobilization) and Hypothesis III, i.e., that involvement in the two political systems will be of analogous form (political syncretism).

Factor analysis is a method of data organization which is widely used for reducing a set of variables to their underlying dimensions of variation. In this study, factor analysis is employed to determine the extent to which the two hypothesized forms of political involvement, modern and syncretistic, exist empirically. First, a principal components analysis was undertaken because this method extracts those dimensions which represent the maximum amount of common variance.[14] Specifically, the first component accounts for the maximum portion of the variance in the data which can be associated with a single linear dimension; the second does the same for the variance which remains; and so on until the total variance is explained. In effect, such a factor matrix allows us to determine the maximum amount of overlap or polarization in variation within the original data matrix. As a result, we will obtain some idea of the upper limits of mobilization and syncretism. Second, a varimax rotation was performed on the principal components matrix. Varimax highlights both those combinations of variables which have a high intercorrelation with each other and individual variables which have very little association with the others. Thus, varimax emphasizes the separateness of items in the original data matrix from the others. Those not having a high association with either a cluster of intercorrelated items or a single variable are given a low factor loading for the dimensions representing a specific cluster or variable. In most cases, the excluded variables achieve a high loading on another factor or have a factor to themselves. For purposes of this study, the resulting varimax matrix will delineate the extent to which the twenty-four political involvement variables may be isolated into separate dimensions. It thus indicates the types of mobilization and syncretism which are most intense in character.

Two aspects of the factor matrices will be of concern in examining the extent to which the political mobilization and syncretism models provide an accurate representation of the data being analyzed. First, each factor itself allows generalization. Where traditional and modern forms of involvement have high loadings with opposite signs, the factor indicates substantial polarization with respect to the two political systems and thus a mobilization effect at least with respect to the political involvement identified. Where either the traditional or modern forms of behavior have high loadings and the other form has a moderate degree of correlation with the factor in the opposite direction, some mobilization can be inferred. Loadings with a similar sign for involvement in both the traditional and modern systems suggest the existence of a syncretistic effect.

Second, especially with varimax, patterns within the factor matrix are also important. The more discrete a factor is (i.e., the more it is based on a variable or variables having very little association with the other factors) the more this factor reflects aspects of political involvement relatively unaffected by the other variables in the original data matrix. Thus, if we find that a general political mobilization factor does not include several of the modern involvement variables, we can suggest some refinement in Hypothesis I, especially if those variables which are not associated appear to be of a particular type. In effect, factor analysis will identify dimensions of political involvement which coexist in a given political structure but have little impact on each other. This coexistence may entail a series of modern participation dimensions which are unrelated to each other as well as several traditional participation dimensions which are neither connected with each other or with the various types of modern involvement. If traditional and modern factors have a highly discrete relation to each other, a form of syncretism is actually occurring; however, this syncretism is different from that in Hypothesis III. In the hypothesis, a single person is postulated as likely to engage in traditional and modern forms of political activity of a similar nature. The coexistence of traditional and modern participation factors, on the other hand, indicates that the local political context includes activity related to the old and new politics *but* that neither mobilization or syncretism are descriptive of the character of political involvement at the individual level. The syncretism is that of a system, not that of the citizen.

PRINCIPAL COMPONENTS ANALYSIS

The analysis of the principal components matrix will only be concerned with the first three dimensions. The remaining components account for a relatively small proportion of the variance, and the analysis which can be derived is better undertaken on the basis of the varimax matrix. The loadings of all seven components are found in Table I.

TABLE I

PRINCIPAL COMPONENTS OF TWENTY-FOUR POLITICAL INVOLVEMENT ITEMS[*]

VARIABLES	I	II	III	IV	V	VI	VII	COMMUNALITIES
1. Extra-local political information	.74							.63
2. Council builds primary schools	.73							.57
3. Council collects taxes	.74							.59
4. Council decides on location of boreholes	.70							.54
5. Council controls the collection of stray cattle	.68							.49
6. President is more powerful than chiefs	.57							.47
7. Land boards better at allocating land	.66							.46
8. MP's more concerned than chiefs	.59							.64
9. Councilmen more concerned than headmen	.60					.46		.52
10. Council unites people better than chief	.60							.58
11. Chief's wisdom should prevail	-.51	-.49	.32			.37		.49
12. Will serve as advisor to chief		-.47	.51					.61
13. Will work with age regiment	-.34	-.42	.49					.67
14. Attends chief's meetings on regular basis		-.42				.38		.41
15. Contacted chief	.30	-.36			.46			.60
16. Concerned about council issue	.39	-.30			.40			.50
17. Contacted councilor	.41	-.42			.44			.62
18. Voted in the last election		-.43	-.31		-.37			.55
19. Party member	.35	-.47	-.35		-.35			.61
20. Attended party rally		-.46		.30	-.30			.59
21. Thought of leaving community				.68				.64
22. Thinks children should live in another community			-.36	.49	.44	-.34		.62
23. Strangers should have equal say with residents						-.34	.81	.85
24. Thinks his point of view considered by leaders			.50				-.30	.47
Percentage of Total Variance Explained by Factor	23.2	7.6	6.2	5.4	5.1	4.9	4.2	56.9
Variance	5.6	1.8	1.5	1.3	1.2	1.2	1.0	

*Respondents with missing data for any pair of variables were excluded from the calculation of the correlation co-
efficient for the two variables. The cutoff for the determination of principal components was an eigenvalue of 1.
Only factor loadings ≥ .30 are included in the matrix.

[20]

The first principal component accounts for almost one-quarter of the total variation in the data. The items probing awareness and evaluation of the change in local government structures (nos. 2-11) have higher loadings than any of the others. In addition, the scale reflecting knowledge of some of the most prominent extra-local political personalities (no. 1) has a very high correlation with this factor. It is thus possible to say that for the items being analyzed, cognizance of and support for the change in the local government structure is the largest single dimension of covariation. More interesting, however, is the relation of the other items to this factor. The five connected with council participation (nos. 16-20) show some association, but it is apparent that such activity cannot be viewed as in any way strongly related to this dimension of awareness and moral support for the change in local government structures. The two intense forms of participation—concern about local council issues and contacting a local councilor—do evidence a somewhat higher relationship than the rest. The five traditional items (nos. 11-15) show a variegated pattern. Two—willingness to cancel a local development project if the chief is opposed and willingness to work with an age regiment upon the chief's command if time permits—show a definite negative relationship to this first component. Such a pattern indicates a definite fissure between those who are aware and supportive of the new government structure and those who are still willing to submit to the chief's directions. The two questions which probe the inclination of the respondent to involve himself in the traditional communication system are almost completely unrelated to this dimension. In effect, an attentive role in the traditional system appears to be taken by Batswana regardless of their awareness and moral evaluation of the new structure. One traditional item—persuasion of a traditional authority—has a definite positive loading on this first dimension. Since this item reflects the most active form of involvement in the traditional polity, it would appear that those who are traditional activists are also likely to be concerned about and possibly supportive of the emergence of the new local government structure. The one set of questions which has little relation to the first factor is that which probes feelings of community cohesion (nos. 21-24). The norms of cohesion which these items reflect are, thus, not of much significance either in a negative or positive sense as far as the mobilization of any awareness of the new government structure or a feeling of support for this change.

This first component does indicate a definite mobilization effect in the sense that all the awareness and moral evaluation items manifest a similar association with this dimension. Also, councilmatic participation does have some positive connection, and several traditional participation items have a negative relation. In short, there is some support for Hypothesis I which concerns political mobilization. It should be noted, however, that this hypothesis does not have as much relevance for participation as for perceptual change. Such a limited scope of items may indicate a potential weakness of studies of political mobilization which do not go beyond the perception level to active forms of involvement. In effect, these studies have not explored those aspects of mass politics where mobilization is less likely to take place.

The second most substantial component of covariation in the data after the extraction of the first is a very general dimension of participation. All the modern and four of the five traditional participation items load between .30 and .49. The fact that none load extremely high signifies that this dimension is composed of a number of clusters of variables but that there is some interrelation among these clusters. The character of the clustering and interconnections will become apparent with rotation. The covariation of the traditional and modern participation items points to a definite overall syncretistic pattern in the data as far as *participation* is concerned. Since the second component represents the maximum amount of variation in the data after the first has been extracted, this second component indicates that participation in council politics is related to traditional participation as well as to the perceptual change reflected in the first component. This participation component, in short, confirms Hypothesis III, i.e., that involvement in the traditional system has a carry-over effect into the modern system. To be sure, it is not possible to be very specific about the character of the carry-over.

The one traditional participation item which has little association with the second dimension is the question concerning the respondent's willingness to have the community go ahead with a development project, like a school, if the chief is opposed. Since this question required a choice between the two polities, at least in the sense of a person being inclined to reject the chief's authority for that of public opinion, it is not surprising that such a form of participation, i.e., standing for or against the chief, did not fall within this syncretistic dimension.

The second component encompasses a set of questions which are different in kind from those which loaded on the first component. Those associated with the latter entailed a choice between the traditional and modern systems: Does the respondent know whether the chief or the council has a specific power, or does he believe officials in one structure are doing a better job in a specific regard than those in the other? The Component II items, on the other hand, require no such choice between the two political systems. Apparently, many are involved in both types of activity, or at least they would prefer to do so if they had a chance. Indeed, the only participation item that did not load on Component II was the one which required a choice between the two systems as far as the type of behavior the respondent would prefer to undertake.

The fact that a participation dimension emerges once the perceptual variation included in Component I is partialled out of the analysis is an indication that perceptual change even to the point of moral commitment does not entail a congruent behavioral change. Such a hiatus between perception and behavior is not a startling finding. Social scientists often note a dissonance between thought and action. In part, the character of Botswana politics facilitates this incongruity. The political party organizations have not very effectively penetrated the local social and economic milieu for the purpose of mobilizing the people to vote, let alone to act as a counter force to the authority of the chief. Those who are inclined towards the new system are thus not very well organized. Indeed, the party activists seek the support of the traditional authorities in lieu of setting up a new organization in some areas. In addition, as was noted above, the chiefs and headmen continue to perform a number of their functions as traditional authorities. Even more important, the people respect them as the symbolic leaders of the community. Thus, it may not pay those who are supportive of the new council structure to totally disregard the traditional political system because the leaders of this system are still a potent political force in the community. Conversely, the traditional elites may see something to be gained from party politicians by encouraging their followers to participate in electoral politics.

The third component in Table I highlights a split between the traditional and modern participation items. Loading on the positive side are some forms of traditional participation. Responses reflecting attachment to the local community, i.e., opposed to children leaving the local community and the belief that one's opinion is considered by community decision makers, also are associated with traditional participation. Having a moderately negative association are voting and party membership. This component appears to give some support to those theorists such as Lerner (1958) who view traditional cohesion as an important influence in the political change process. From this perspective, personalized contacts, especially those within the family or within an ethnic group, are the basis for political communication, the linkage for authority structures, and the determinants of the nature and extent of popular participation. The rupture of such ties and the emergence of a sense of psychic mobility make possible citizen involvement in the modern system.

This component provides some evidence for the existence at the participation level of a polarization effect entailed in Hypothesis I. It will be remembered that the first component identified a perception change which has a mobilizing connection with participation in both the traditional and councilmatic realms. In essence, principal components analysis suggests the possibility of two types of participation mobilization supporting Hypothesis I: that which is associated with perceptual change and that which accompanies the breaking of bonds with the traditional community.

Most pertinent about the principal components analysis is the fact that both the political mobilization and syncretism hypotheses are verified depending on the data emphasized. With no controls introduced, the first component highlighted the strong association among the perception variables and their limited mobilizing impact on participation in the traditional and councilmatic systems. When this factor was partialled out of the analysis, a syncretistic pattern for participation emerged. Then, controlling for both these dimensions, a polarization effect was evident among the participation variables—in this case connected with a persistence or absence of a sense of local political community. In short, the two hypotheses are not so much mutually exclusive as dependent on the type of citizen involvement being considered.

VARIMAX

The principal components analysis employed in the foregoing discussion creates a set of dimensions which explain the maximum amount of variance in the original data matrix. Such dimensions, however, are very dependent on the mix of variables selected for inclusion in a study. If, for instance, there were only a few perception questions, the character of the components might have been considerably different. Rotation of the principal components matrix is undertaken to secure a solution which is more invariant. As we have noted above, a rotated solution achieves this effect by giving a high loading on a factor to those variables which have a particularly high correlation with each other. The factors are invariant in that so long as a cluster of variables which load high on a factor in one study is included in the data matrix of another study carried out under similar conditions, the same factor will very likely reappear in the rotated matrix, even though the other variables being examined may change substantially in the second study (Rummel, 1970: 369-385). The varimax method also has the advantage of producing factors which are completely uncorrelated. Each dimension is statistically unique from the others. Thus, this approach tends to maximize the extent to which the original data can be isolated into separate realms of behavior.[15]

The results of the varimax rotation are presented in Table II. The first two factors break down the questions related to awareness and evaluation of the local government change (nos. 2-6 and 7-10 respectively) into two separate dimensions. Factor I, which highlights awareness of the legal change, shows some association with three out of the five modern participation items (nos. 16, 17, 20), including the two more intense forms of participation which entail concern over local issues and contacting a local councilor. On the other hand, Factor II, which reflects a positive moral position toward the new council system, evidences much less association with these same modern participation items. Instead, this factor has a negative correlation with the very participation items which have the strongest connection with the legal awareness factor. At least for the behavior being considered in this study, moral commitment to the modern structure is not associated with a dramatic upsurge of participation in politics related to this structure.

The basis for such a pattern cannot be explored very extensively with the present data. One possible explanation is suggested by the political community question probing the respondent's perception as to whether local leaders consider his point of view. Those who are aware of the change (Factor I) tend to feel in fairly substantial numbers that their opinions are considered (.49); those who support the new council structure (Factor II) are inclined in the opposite direction though to a lesser extent (-.16). It would appear that moral support for the new political structure tends to come from those who are somewhat alienated from local political decisions, even though many of these decisions have been made in recent years by the council. For such citizens, the councils may appear more effective because of the control which the national government is able to exercise over council policy making. In fact, one function of the local councilors is to explain national policies to the people (Holm, 1972: 85). Thus, these supporters of the transformation in local government identified in Factor II may not perceive their own participation as very significant in determining council behavior but believe that the councils are moving in the right direction anyway. Also, as was mentioned above, these modernizers may not be very effectively mobilized by local party organizations. Indeed, they may even be highly suspicious of the

TABLE II

VARIMAX FACTORS OF TWENTY-FOUR POLITICAL INVOLVEMENT ITEMS*

VARIABLES	FACTORS							COMMUNALITIES
	I	II	III	IV	V	VI	VII	
1. Extra-local political information	(.71)	.11	.17	.27	-.07	-.02	.02	.63
2. Council builds primary schools	(.69)	.25	.12	.10	-.09	.01	.08	.58
3. Council collects taxes	(.71)	.25	.06	.14	-.09	.00	.05	.60
4. Council decides on location of boreholes	(.67)	.27	.07	.06	-.04	.03	.02	.53
5. Council controls collection of stray cattle	(.61)	.28	.02	.17	-.10	.05	.07	.50
6. President more powerful than chiefs	(.61)	.19	.18	-.07	.15	-.03	-.01	.47
7. Land Boards better at allocating land	(.53)	.34	-.11	.12	-.16	.11	.00	.46
8. MP's more concerned than chiefs	.32	(.73)	-.04	.06	.00	-.02	-.05	.64
9. Councilmen more concerned than headmen	.39	(.58)	.06	-.01	-.03	-.11	.05	.51
10. Council unites people better than chief	.31	(.69)	.03	.03	-.09	.00	.04	.58
11. Chief's wisdom should prevail	-.15	-.46	.24	-.22	.36	-.14	.00	.49
12. Will serve as advisor to the chief	.06	-.02	.09	.03	(.77)	.02	.06	.61
13. Will work with age regiment	-.18	-.13	-.13	.01	(.74)	.03	-.08	.62
14. Attends chief's meetings on regular basis	-.26	.24	.17	.15	.43	.13	.18	.41
15. Contacted chief	-.01	.22	.04	(.74)	.08	.03	-.03	.60
16. Concerned about council issue	.32	-.12	.08	(.61)	-.06	.05	.07	.50
17. Contacted councilor	.22	-.01	.13	(.74)	.01	.01	.06	.61
18. Voted in last election	.05	.06	(.67)	.07	-.08	.01	.27	.55
19. Party member	.08	.08	(.73)	.19	-.07	.11	-.05	.61
20. Attended party rally	.27	-.09	(.66)	.02	.19	.13	-.12	.59
21. Thought of leaving community	.05	.02	.12	-.03	.05	(-.76)	.18	.64
22. Thinks children should live in another community	.10	.00	.16	.04	-.10	(-.75)	-.14	.63
23. Strangers should have equal say with residents	.07	.00	.02	-.03	.01	-.02	(.92)	.85
24. Thinks his point of view considered by leaders	.49	-.16	-.24	-.06	.08	.29	.20	.46
Percentage of Total Variance Explained	28.7	16.0	13.0	12.7	11.8	9.7	8.1	

*Factor loadings ≥ .50 are in parentheses.

traditional status of many local party officials. Therefore, they are not attracted to the new forms of participation being examined in this study.

Both Factors I and II show substantial negative association with a number of the traditional participation items. In this sense, they confirm the political mobilization hypothesis. The pattern of the moral factor (II) is, however, significantly conflicting. As might be expected, it has a very strong negative correlation with the response which indicates a willingness to defer to the chief's rejection of a project even if the community is generally favorable. In short, those who support the council system depreciate the legitimacy of traditional authority. On the other hand, they seem to feel a definite need to participate in the traditional communications system. This commitment is evidenced by the positive association of Factor II with a willingness to both advise the chief and to attend public meetings which he calls.

The grounds for such behavior are not completely clear. One very possible explanation is that those who support the new council structure believe that the chief and his subordinates remain a most effective means for communicating with the mass of the population. Even the socialist oriented founders of the Botswana National Front (BNF), the fastest growing opposition party in the late sixties, very openly recognized this fact of Tswana political life and thus sought to forge an alliance with traditional authorities in order to secure a mass following (Koma). The respondents in this study, then, may be participating in the traditional communications system in order to influence and monitor the messages the chief gives to his followers within the local populace. In effect, the syncretism at the mass level may in part involve persons alienated from the traditional structures making use of the traditional authorities for promoting change.

The third, fourth and fifth factors in the varimax solution divide nine of the ten participation items into three dimensions: mass electoral participation (III), intense participation (IV), and traditional mass participation (V). In effect, the variation involved in Component II above is broken down into three separate factors. The only major confirmation of the political syncretism hypothesis which remains is the intense participation factor. Those who are inclined towards more intense forms of activity tend to do so both in the traditional and modern systems. To be sure, this pattern may be mostly the result of crossover by supporters of one of the two structures to the other. Thus far, our examination of factor loadings has only indicated that persons morally favorable to the council system are inclined also to persuade the chief. Other influences may also be involved which indicate that traditional interests are being pursued within the modern structure through intense participation.

The orthogonal character of varimax establishes each of the three participation dimensions as being uncorrelated to the others. This effect could have been imposed by the rotation method; however, the high loading variables on each factor do not show much association with the other two. Thus, involvement in any one of these participation dimensions tends to be quite unrelated to a consistent choice concerning engagement in the other two. This indicates that the political syncretism of Component II above is of a very limited extent. To be sure, within local politics these three forms of participation support the existence of both traditional and councilmatic authority structures which interact with each other. In this respect, the three dimensions of participation facilitate syncretism at the elite level.

The emergence of two separate dimensions for electoral and traditional mass participation (Factors III and IV) shows that the political mobilization hypothesis has little relevance to the variables which load high on these two factors; namely, modes of participation which tend to be of low intensity. At least in Botswana, it would be dangerous to assume that an increase in electoral forms of activity is inversely related with citizen willingness to continue traditional forms of low intensity participation. Such a factor pattern may be the result of the fact that Botswana politics has thus far entailed fairly open recognition by traditional and modern elites of the legitimacy of both systems of mass involvement. Many elected politicians have traditional status and often seek the support of traditional authorities. On the other hand, the chiefs are encouraged and generally have agreed to work both with the new national government through the House of Chiefs and with the councils by serving as their presiding officers. In short, the political structure has not been one which stimulated people to think in terms of a definitive choice between the traditional and modern systems. This detente could explain why the electoral and traditional participation dimensions coexist with neither having much effect on the other. The political mobilization hypothesis may require a much higher conflict level between supporters of the two systems of authority.

None of the three participation dimensions would appear to be a very good predictor of the mass reaction to such a conflict. The one participation question which asked the respondents to choose between the traditional and modern systems (no. 11) loads on all three participation factors to a moderate extent. This question concerned the willingness of Batswana to support their chief's rejection of a project approved by the community as a whole. The traditional participants showed a willingness to support the chief while those involved in electoral activities and the intense participants were somewhat inclined to go ahead regardless of the chief's opposition. It would appear that neither the traditional nor the modern political structures has very substantial legitimacy among the citizens participating in each.

The final two factors in Table II relate to the community cohesion items. Factor VI focuses on what might be termed psychic mobility (Lerner, 1958). The two high loading items concern whether the respondent has thought of moving to another community and whether he thinks his children should raise their offspring in another community. Factor VII emphasizes parochialism. This factor's only strongly correlating variable probes whether people moving into the respondent's community should have an equal say with longtime residents.

The appearance of separate varimax factors for the cohesion items indicates the relative independence of these dimensions from the variation identified by the other factors. This separateness is further highlighted by the fact that the specific variables composing the two cohesion factors show very little correlation with the other five dimensions in the matrix. In effect, the aspects of political community reflected by the three items have minimal association with transformations in the other realms of political activity being considered. It was noted above that principal components analysis showed some support for the thesis that political mobilization within the modern system is associated with a breaking of bonds an individual has with the traditional community. This process does not appear to be very extensive; otherwise, it would have persisted within the varimax rotation.

One very possible explanation for the minimal effect of community cohesion within either of the political structures is that these variables have never been important elements in determining political community in Botswana politics. Traditionally, political loyalty was primarily determined by a person or kinship group swearing allegiance to a chief and the concomitant acceptance of the individual or group by the chief concerned. In some cases persons from other tribes have been given positions of substantial leadership by the chief to whom they have transferred their loyalty because of the extraordinary way in which this loyalty was demonstrated, e.g., leadership or bravery in war. It has also been common practice for kinship groupings as large as a clan to move from one tribal area to another as a result of an unresolved political conflict in the community in which they originally lived. All of the Tswana tribes contain kinship units which have migrated from other areas and these migrants have, for the most part, the same political rights as other community members (Schapera, 1952). Thus, it is not likely because of traditional political culture for a Motswana who moves to another political community to be looked on as an outsider for purposes of political decision-making, regardless of whether the traditional or modern system is involved.

The more stringent variable association criteria required by the varimax rotation limit the scope of mobilization and syncretism with respect to mass political involvement within Botswana local politics. Two types of association appear most likely to be invariant, and therefore transcend this case study, with respect to hypotheses I and III. In particular, the political mobilization thesis is reflected in Factor I by the legal awareness items which in addition to their association with each other also go along with an inclination to participate in some aspects of councilmatic politics and some aversion to traditional mass activities. On the other hand, Factor IV confirms the political syncretism hypothesis in that the same persons tend to be inclined toward the most active forms of citizen participation in both the traditional and modern structures.

The most consistent finding in the varimax matrix is the lack of evidence for a strong trend reflecting either of the two hypotheses. The legal awareness items of Factor I have only a moderate association with participation in the new council system and a slight connection with the traditional participation items. Moral support for the new council structure in Factor II shows more connection with the traditional communication system than with any of the council participation items. Such a pattern may indicate that at least in Botswana those who have been mobilized to support the modern system are actually more likely to participate in the traditional system even though their commitment is to the modern system. In sum, the effect presented in this factor is just the reverse of that postulated by the political mobilization hypotheses. Factors III, IV and V also all show the weakness of both hypotheses for explaining Tswana behavior. None evidence a very strong association with any of the variables requiring a choice between the two systems, thus reflecting the limited extent of the mobilization hypothesis. In addition, the only confirmation of syncretism among these factors is at the most active level of mass involvement; the more passive forms of mass behavior, i.e., the variables loading on Factors III and V, show almost no association with each other, which would be expected for political syncretism, or with the one dimension confirming syncretism, i.e., Factor IV.

In assessing the limited extent to which the varimax pattern confirms the political mobilization and syncretism hypotheses, a number of explanations have been offered. In their specific forms, these explanations suggest the more general contention that the emergence of political mobilization or syncretism in specific mass involvement dimensions depends on the character of the past and present political structure. The following particular arguments have been made to support this proposition: that moral support for the local political structure may not be translated into direct contacts with the local council if the national government is more receptive to the ideas of those supporting the new local structure than the local officials manning this structure; that this more mobilized group may perceive the Tswana Chiefs to be the most effective manipulators of local public opinion and thus the most important officials at the local level to be influenced or countered; that the competition between traditional and modern elites may not be sufficiently manifest to generate a mobilization effect in terms of participation; and that the Tswana sense of political community with respect to kinship groups and stranger participation in politics has been of a character which is congruent with the new council structure of politics as well as traditional forms of involvement.

COMPONENT VERSUS FACTOR DIMENSIONS

The two factor matrixes we have just examined shed different perspectives on the pattern of mass involvement in the traditional and modern political structures in Botswana. It will be remembered that prior to the survey five dimensions of local participation were postulated:

(1) legal awareness of the change in local government structures;
(2) moral support for this change;
(3) participation in the new council structures;
(4) participation in the traditional political structures; and
(5) a sense of traditional political community.

The virtue of the principal components analysis is that it highlights the most inclusive patterns of mobilization and syncretism among these five sets of variables. Specifically, the component concerned with awareness and evaluation of the new council system evidenced a general perceptual mobilization as well as some polarization effect with respect to modern and traditional participation; the component including all the participation items reflected political syncretism; and the component which brought a number of traditional participation and political community items together showed some polarization with modern participation items. The varimax rotation, on the other hand, emphasized the extent to which the originally postulated five sets of variables could be separated into dimensions unrelated to each other. The result was confirmation of four of the postulated realms of involvement *plus* the extraction of an additional one concerned with intense participation and the separation of political cohesion into two dimensions. The extent of political mobilization and syncretism was minimized. The former remained only in the connection between the legal awareness items and a slight tendency toward increased modern participation and decreased traditional involvement; the latter in the covariance of activism in the two political structures.

In examining the relationship between the twenty-four political involvement items and socio-economic change, the varimax factors will be more appropriate to use in developing factor scores for the respondents than the principal components. The former has the advantage of isolating one form of involvement from another more than is the case with the latter. The analysis is not clouded by the need to assess in one operation the differential impact of the independent variables on various aspects of political change. For instance, rather than having an index that ranges from traditional to modern participation, as would be the case with the third principal component, varimax identifies three separate dimensions, one for intense participation, another for electoral activity and a third for traditional mass participation. It will thus be possible with the varimax dimensions to compare the extent to which the socio-economic variables having a particular effect on one of these political dimensions have an opposite or similar connection with the other two.

VI. THE SOCIO-ECONOMIC STRUCTURE AND POLITICAL PARTICIPATION

According to social mobilization theory, certain modernizing changes in the socio-economic environment are associated with or actually induce the emergence of modern types of political activity among the general populace. The character of the socio-economic change is delineated in numerous ways. Some studies concentrate on a limited number of factors, such as education and mass media exposure, which are relatively easy to quantify and often can be shown to have a definite effect (Goel, 1970; McCrone and Cnudde, 1967). Other inquiries combine a number of specific forms of change into one or several comprehensive variables, such as class composition and interest group membership (Nie et al., 1969). Still others examine a whole range of social and economic variables which are considered to be part of the modernization process (Deutsch, 1961; Inkeles, 1969). The problem is that as the number of variables is expanded, the assessment of the relation of each to dependent political variables becomes increasingly complicated or impossible to identify. Particularly difficult are the problems of analysis which arise from intercorrelation and interaction among the various socio-economic variables (Morgan and Sonquist, 1963). Social mobilization theory is based on the assumption that both these effects occur. It is presumed: (1) that the modernization process consists of a number of concomitant changes (intercorrelation) and (2) that these changes have a stimulating effect on each other and thus result in a greater cumulative impact on change in political thought and behavior than would be the consequence of each change working separately (interaction).

Both these problems are further complicated by syncretistic theory. This theory postulates that the social mobilization variables are intertwined with already existing socio-economic stimuli in determining the extent and character of political change. From the syncretistic perspective certain groups in the population, say the royalist clan or a particular tribe, will be inclined because of cultural norms or their economic circumstance to reject or adopt various forms of socio-economic modernization (intercorrelation). Also, the consequences of socio-economic modernization for political change may be inhibited or accelerated by norms or economic opportunities existing in the traditional context (interaction).

The most significant relationship for this paper is that of various *associations* of the socio-economic variables from the two models of political change with specific forms of mass political activity and thought delineated in the previous section. For parsimony of analysis it is best to combine those parameters of socio-economic context that are highly correlated into as few indices of the total extra-political influence as are feasible. The discussion which follows is based on a set of dimensions of social and economic structure created by a factor analysis of an original data matrix containing 21 social and economic variables. The resulting 7 factors reflect just over two-thirds (64%) of the total variation in this matrix. While one-third of the total variation is excluded from consideration, the dimensions derived include a number which are very salient to mobilization and syncretistic theory.

The original 21 variables are listed in Exhibit B. After each variable the categories into which it is divided are enumerated. The 21 variables

EXHIBIT B

TWENTY-ONE ORIGINAL SOCIO-ECONOMIC VARIABLES

Items Included	Possible Responses
1. Place of Residence	Rural/ Urban
2. Sex	Female/ Male
3. Age	20-29/ 30-39/ 40-49/ 50-59/ 60-69/ 70-79/ 80 and over
4. Source of food	All purchased in the market/ Partial dependence on family production*
5. Religion	Never a Christian/ Presently or formerly a Christian
6. Education	Number of years
7. Newspaper reading	Almost daily/ two or three times a week/ once a week/ never
8. Radio Listening	Almost daily/ two or three times a week/ once a week/ never
9. Family cultivates some fields	No/ Yes
10. Family raises cattle	No/ Yes
11. Family member earns income in Government	No/ Yes
12. Family member employed in private sector	No/ Yes
13. Family member self-employed	No/ Yes
14. Respondent has migrated to South Africa to labor	No/ Yes
15. Time spent as a labor migrant	Number of years
16. Respondent's spouse has migrated to South Africa to labor	No/ Yes
17. Time spouse spent as a labor migrant	Number of years
18. Number of cattle owned	25 or less/ more than 25**
19. Status in traditional society	Commoner or stranger/ royal clan
20. Respondent presently a wage earner	No/ Yes
21. Spouse presently a wage earner	No/ Yes

*Almost all Tswana must depend on market purchases to survive because the arid climate makes subsistence production extremely difficult.

**See Appendix I for a discussion of why this variable was dichotomized.

used here combine two qualities: (1) They are reflective of generally accepted socio-economic components of mobilization theory in the contemporary literature or of politically significant aspects of the traditional Tswana social structure; and (2) A question could be formulated in such a way as to provide reasonable probability of a reliable response within the Botswana context.[16] The socio-economic factors were derived from a varimax rotation of a principal components analysis of the original data matrix. [17] The varimax factor loadings are presented in Table II of the Appendix. The first factor is a general social mobilization factor having education, newspaper reading and radio listening as its high loading variables and wage-earning, connection with the church, government occupation, urbanization, youth and ownership of over 25 head of cattle as moderate loadings. This dimension clearly indicates an association of the modern communications with Christianity and various forms of involvement in the market economy ranging from government employment to rural cattle holding. The next five factors are related to specific aspects of Tswana economic life. Factor II concerns involvement in rural economy specifically including partial subsistence existence, cultivation of fields, cattle raising, and ownership of over 25 cattle. Factor III focuses on migration of the respondent's spouse to South Africa for labor. Factor IV deals with migration of the respondent himself to South Africa for the same purpose. Salient to both these factors are two variables; one establishing whether migration has occurred and the other the number of years involved. Factors V and VI concentrate on only one variable each: private employment and self-employment respectively. The last factor emphasizes the distinction between royal clan membership and commoner status in traditional Tswana society. It reflects an association of royal status with several variables generally conducive to active participation in the traditional political system; namely, rural residence and seniority of age. That traditional status should rank higher than these other variables is most useful to our subsequent analysis in that, as has already been noted, such status more than any other variable always assured those possessing it of the right to make their opinions known to the chief, except in the case of royal females being excluded from some policy discussions.[18]

In order to establish the relationship between these socio-economic factors and the seven political involvement dimensions identified in the earlier varimax rotation, factor scores were calculated for each respondent for both sets of factors.[19] A multiple regression analysis of each political involvement factor with the seven socio-economic factors was then undertaken. Since the socio-economic factors created by varimax are uncorrelated with each other, the beta coefficients in the regression equation indicate the relative strength of association of each of these independent variables with the political involvement dimension being considered. In such circumstances, the betas are equivalent to correlation coefficients for the individual socio-economic factors with the dependent variable. By squaring either the beta or the correlation coefficient for each of the socio-economic factors with a particular involvement factor and adding the results together, it is possible to obtain the total variance explained by a multiple regression equation.

The hypotheses to be considered in this section concern the general pattern of relationship between socio-economic structure and political change. They are hypotheses II and IV from the first section of this paper:

> Hypothesis II—Citizens who have experienced specific forms of socio-economic modernization are more likely than those who have not experienced such modernization to become involved in modern political structures.

Hypotheses IV—Traditional and modern socio-economic variables
are associated with citizen involvement in either the
traditional or modern political structures.

Most important in regard to these hypotheses is an identification of
the socio-economic factors which are "modern" and those which are
"traditional."[20] Modern will be assumed to pertain to those elements
of Tswana society associated with the cash economy and externally
induced social mobilization phenomena, including Western education,
newspapers, radio, and Christianity. Traditional involves salient
attributes of Tswana society existent before the coming of European
colonial rule. On the basis of these definitions, it is quite apparent that
Factor I falls in the modern category, isolating the most pervasive
extent of social mobilization, and the Factor VII focuses on aspects of
social status salient to traditional Tswana political activity. Among the
remaining five factors, all limited to economic considerations, the
division is not as decisive. It seems reasonable to conclude that private
employment, migration to South Africa, and spouse's migration to
South Africa indicate definite involvement in the cash economy and
thus are modern. Self-employment certainly entails entry into the cash
economy too; however, some of the occupations subsumed under this
category are highly traditional, such as the practice of Tswana
medicine or women selling the local beer. In the case of Factor II,
which concerns various aspects of rural economic existence, the
situation is also difficult to assess. This factor includes both subsistence
farming and some sale of goods in the market. Even relatively poor
Batswana will sell one or several head of cattle in order to cover a major
financial need, such as paying tuition for a child to attend school or
purchasing food in time of drought. Those receiving the highest scores
on this dimension are mostly persons with over 25 head of cattle. While
the possession of such a herd enhances their status traditionally, many
who have large herds are becoming ranchers who sell a portion of their
herd each year. Such Batswana are very much engaged in the
expanding market exchange system which is hypothesized in
mobilization theory to have an impact on political behavior.

The assessment of the character of both the self-employment and
rural economic involvement factors is, thus, unclear. To simplify the
analysis which follows, controls will be introduced for these two factors.
In the case of self-employment, a division of the sample will be made in
terms of sex. The self-employed males tend to be engaged in new
occupations stimulated by the market economy. The females, on the
other hand, are almost all engaged in selling beer. While they are

continuing a traditional role in Tswana society, in the rural areas in particular they are doing so in a form which is clearly more involved in the cash economy than those females who only make beer for family and friends. In the case of the rural economic involvement factor, respondents with more than 25 cattle will be excluded so that an assessment can be made of the extent to which a rural subsistence existence, or the lack thereof, has an impact on change in mass political behavior.

In summary, the seven socio-economic factors may be categorized as follows: Two, I and VII, reflect the polar extremes of social mobilization and a traditional social basis for political participation. Three, factors III, IV, and V, focus on economic forms of mobilization which are not connected with the other socio-economic indicators of modernization; these isolated dimensions are concerned with migration of the respondent himself or his spouse to South Africa and private employment in Botswana. The remaining two factors, II and VI, constitute some connection with the cash economy but clearly also entail traditional social and economic relations. These latter two will be examined under controls which will highlight the impact of either the market economy or traditional relations.

ANALYSIS

Table III contains beta weights for the seven socio-economic factors as independent variables in regression equations calculated for predicting the variation of a number of the political involvement dimensions created by the varimax rotation in the previous section.[21] As noted above in this section, the beta weights indicate the relative importance of specific independent variables in explaining the variation of a dependent variable in a regression equation. Thus, the betas in Table III tell us the relative strength of association of the various socio-economic factors with each of the political dimensions in the table.

Five of the seven political involvement factors identified by varimax rotation in the previous section have been included in Table III. Those excluded relate to psychic mobility and parochialism. Both are not considered here because their connection with traditional political behavior at the mass level was given minimal significance by the varimax rotation. For purposes of testing hypotheses II and IV, it seemed better to concentrate on those aspects of mass involvement which are clearly within traditional politics.

TABLE III

BETA WEIGHTS FOR SEVEN SOCIO-ECONOMIC FACTORS IN REGRESSION EQUATIONS WITH EACH POLITICAL INVOLVEMENT FACTOR*

	legal awareness	moral support	electoral part	intense part	traditional part
1. Modern Social Mobilization	.56	.23	.05	.26	-.12
2. Labor Migration to South Africa	-.01(.05)	-.09	-.18	.05	.13
3. Labor Migration to South Africa (Spouse)	.00	-.01	.18	-.02	.03
4. Private Employment	-.10(.13)	-.04	.04	-.08	.02
5. Rural Economic Involvement	-.10(.07)	.14	.10	.07	.05
6. Self-employment	-.05	-.02	.16	.01	.05
7. Traditional Social Status	-.05	.05	.07(.04)	.17	.06
8. Multiple Correlation Coefficient	.58**	.31**	.33**	.34**	.21**

*The numbers in parentheses are correlation coefficients of a socio-economic variable with a political change factor where the beta for a particular association is more than .02 away from the corresponding correlation coefficient. See note 21 for an explanation of the cause of the effect.

**Significant at ≤ .001

Three types of political involvement factors are examined in Table III. The first three—awareness of the legal change in local government power, moral support for this change, and participation in the local council electoral system—are solely concerned with increasing involvement in the new or modern political structure. The last, traditional participation, reflects customary political behavior. The fourth, intense participation, is a syncretistic dimension relating to both traditional and modern political structures.

In analyzing Table III, the pattern of the beta weights for the various socio-economic factors with each political factor is the essential consideration for testing the hypotheses of socio-economic mobilization and syncretism. The former hypothesis requires a pattern wherein:

(1) the modern social mobilization factors (I, III, IV, and V) have a positive association with one of the modern political involvement factors (I, II, and III) or a negligible or negative relation with traditional participation (V); and

(2) the traditional status factor (VII) and rural economic involvement (II), especially with owners of over 25 head of cattle excluded from the sample, show an insignificant or negative connection with a specific modern political involvement factor or a positive association with traditional participation.

The hypothesis of socio-economic syncretism requires a correlation pattern wherein involvement in either the traditional or modern political dimension has a positive relation with socio-economic factors which are both traditional and modern.

Political Involvement Factor IV, intense participation, already has been established as syncretistic in terms of the political syncretism hypothesis. In this section we will be concerned with the extent to which its socio-economic basis is also syncretistic, or seems to arise from a social mobilization effect. The specifications for such a determination are the same as those in the above paragraph. It is possible that social mobilization could stimulate similar involvement in both systems. We have already noted in the previous section that some of those who were morally supportive of the council system took an activist role in the traditional system in terms of contacting the chief.

Before a detailed analysis is undertaken of specific political involvement dimensions, several general aspects of Table III should be noted. As a group, the socio-economic factors evidence considerable difference in capacity to explain the variance in the seven political dimensions. The most effective explanation is the almost 36% achieved for the awareness of legal change factor. In the case of traditional participation, the socio-economic factors do not achieve 5%. For moral approval of the council structure, mass electoral participation, and intense participation, the proportion ranges around 10%. Thus, with respect to the political dimensions being examined in this section, the seven socio-economic factors are relatively ineffective in explaining the respondents' involvement in the traditional political system, somewhat more successful in probing modern involvement which goes beyond mere awareness, and most precise in delineating the variations in awareness of the legal changes occurring.

Second, the relative importance of the various socio-economic factors in explaining the variation in the political involvement dimensions differs markedly from one form of political involvement to another. The greatest variation is evident in the general social mobilization factor which ranges from a coefficient of .56 for the legal awareness factor to .05 for electoral participation. The traditional status factor has much less of a range, yet it reaches from a coefficient of .17 in the case of intense participation to a -.05 for legal awareness. As will be observed below, this variation expands even further in certain subgroups. The magnitude of the differentials is clearly substantial enough to establish the necessity for a separate consideration of the various dimensions of involvement in analyses of the socio-economic basis for change at the citizen level of politics.

The five political involvement dimensions will now be examined separately. The analysis will not only be concerned with the sample as a whole but with subgroups which make additional explanation possible.[22]

Awareness of Legal Change

This factor has some associations with the socio-economic variables which confirm the socio-economic mobilization hypothesis. Not only does the general social mobilization factor evidence a high correlation (.56) with an awareness of legal change in local government structures; but the rural economic participation factor has a slight *negative* association of .10. Within the urban subsample, the rural economic factor has an even more substantial negative coefficient of .17 with awareness of the new government. And, not surprisingly, the traditional social status factor has almost no significance for legal awareness. The remaining socio-economic factors do not show any support for the socio-economic mobilization hypothesis. The supposedly modern forms of economic involvement—the two related to South African labor migration and the one concerned with private employment in Botswana—have no connection with the awareness factor. Private employment actually has a significant, though very small, negative relationship.

By subsample analysis, a more precise view of the role of labor migration can be obtained. The conventional wisdom is that migrants to a more developed social and economic system such as South Africa are sufficiently mobilized by their experience so that they are more likely than those of otherwise similar circumstance who remain at home to become involved in modern political structures (e.g., Miller, 1966: 193-194). Some scholars have noted an opposite effect. For instance, Skinner (1960: 393) observed that the Mossi migrants returning to Upper Volta from Ghana during the late fifties had difficulty adjusting to changes which had occurred in their absence and were inclined to be among the more conservative in their villages. The main body of migrants in Botswana are males; therefore, this subsample will be examined. Among rural males, Skinner's reverse mobilization thesis is supported in that the correlation of the migration factor with legal awareness is -.20. In the two urban areas of Botswana, the relationship for the male subsample tends toward a slight socio-economic mobilization with a coefficient of .13. It would appear that migration has some mobilizing effect with respect to awareness only among citizens who possess the skills or desire to live and work in the new towns as a consequence of their sojourn in South Africa. Otherwise, working in South Africa tends to cut migrants off from communications which would inform them of the changes which have occurred in local government.

Moral Support for the Council Structure

This factor has much less of a socio-economic mobilization connection than was the case with legal awareness. The modern social mobilization factor only has a beta of .23—in the towns it goes up to .34. All three of the modernizing economic factors have a negligible relation to this dimension. Indeed, in the urban areas, the co-efficient for labor migrants is a -.19 in contract to the positive beta of .13 which we noted above for the legal awareness factor. Whatever social-economic mobilization is involved in labor migration for those in the towns, it does not seem to carry over from the realm of awareness of the changes to moral support for the council structure. Rather, the reaction seems to be more one of rejection from this structure or at least alienation.

Some evidence of socio-economic syncretism is apparent in that moral support of the council structure also shows a positive correlation (.14) with involvement in the rural economy. Those who stay at home and work within the confines of the traditional social structure in the rural areas are more likely to support the council system than those who go to South Africa and then return to Botswana, even if they come back to the urban areas. Given the arbitrary manner in which many Tswana chiefs and headmen have handled questions of land tenure, it is quite possible that persons who are most dependent on agricultural production are inclined to perceive a definite need to strip the chief of his powers and turn this authority over to the new councils. The possible connection of market involvement with such a reaction is indicated by the fact that when the owners of over 25 head of cattle are removed from the sample, the beta for rural economic involvement drops from .14 to .07.

Particularly significant as far as the connection between rural economic involvement and moral support for the council is the rural female population in which the correlation is .27. In contrast, rural males have a beta of -.08. In other words, rural males tend to be opposed to the new council structure. The basis for this difference is not completely clear, but it may well be related to the character of the traditional power structure: In most instances, females are excluded from having a say in political discussions, including the allocation of land, except through their spouse. Without a husband, they are likely to rely on their father or brothers if such are available and willing to help. In the case of the council, on the other hand, women have an equal opportunity to vote and lobby with decision makers, and they are already known for having done so in most councils. Since somewhere around a quarter of the Tswana families may be fatherless and another group have husbands away in South Africa working, there is a substantial body of women who are excluded from the traditional political process as far as using their husband. The council has an added attraction for these women in that it is associated with the national government's Food For Work Program through which the poor are able to earn food in return for labor on village projects. Some evidence of this effect is provided by the fact that among rural females the beta for rural economic involvement's connection with moral support for the council structure only drops from .27 for the group as a whole to a still respectable .20 for those with 25 or less cattle.

Electoral Participation

This factor evidences very little support for either of the hypotheses being studied in this section. The modern social mobilization factor only has a slight positive beta for the association with electoral participation. Even among the subgroup of urban residents, its relation is a minimal .13. With rural males the impact of modern social mobilization is actually slightly negative. Traditional social status also shows only a very slight positive association of .07 for the total sample. Among a subsample of rural males with 25 or less cattle, the correlation reached .14, hardly an indication of substantial syncretism.

Most striking is the lack of a definite impact by the modern social mobilization factor. In the two dimensions of political involvement previously discussed, social mobilization was by far the socio-economic factor with the strongest relationship to political change. Apparently the respondents' perceptual mobilization in terms of awareness of a change and moral support for the change has not yet carried over into the realm of electoral participation. To put the matter another way, if perception change results in behavior modification, it does not appear in this case to be as consequence of the concomitant impact of social mobilization on these various domains of political involvement. Needless to say, this substantial difference in the importance of modern social mobilization for the three dimensions of political change we have thus far examined is confirmation of the necessity to look at a range of forms of political involvement in testing any theory concerning political modernization at the level of citizen politics. It is quite possible that with a more developed economy than currently exists in Botswana, social mobilization might be more substantial.[23] Lerner (1958: 64), for instance, suggests that a high rate of voting requires substantial previous urbanization, literacy and economic development.[24] Also, the correlation might be greater if a democratic structure had existed for a longer period of time[25] or if the parties competing for power had little sympathy for or identification with the traditional political structure.

With the exception of private employment, the economic factors have a more substantial connection with the dependent political variable of electoral participation than either general social mobilization or traditional social status. The pattern of correlations, especially among subgroups, would seem to suggest that involvement in electoral activity is somewhat tied to the *intensity* of participation in the rural market economy. Such a pattern is a confirmation of socio-economic mobilization hypothesis in that engaging in the cash economy accompanies increased political involvement. One indication of this effect is that among rural males, the rural economic involvement factor has a .18 association with the electoral activities factor. The effect of intensity of economic involvement is particularly manifested by the drop of the beta weight to .08 when those with more than 25 head of cattle are removed from the rural male subsample. Another case of this intensity effect is among the subsample of rural females where the self-employment factor obtains a correlation of .20 with electoral involvement. As was observed above, the most substantial group of rural females who are self-employed are those selling beer. They have translated their role of making beer for family and friends into a market activity. They are thus more involved in the cash economy than their female neighbors who rely in most cases on their husbands for a cash income. One final piece of evidence of intensity of rural economic involvement being associated with higher electoral participation is the behavior of spouses of migrants. While the rural economic involvement factor has a negative beta of .10 for the rural female subsample, the spouses of migrants factor has a positive correlation of .18. The wives of migrants must of necessity be more involved in economic life of the family than those who have their husbands at home. It would not seem unlikely, thus, that spouses of migrants would look to the new political system, where they are accepted on a more equal basis than in the traditional structure, as one context in which to protect their economic interests.

Evidence of the impact of a low intensity of rural economic involvement, the other side of the coin from that discussed in the previous paragraph, is provided by the negative connection (.18) of labor migration with electoral participation (see Table III). Those who go to South Africa to earn part of their income clearly do not, on the whole, have to depend on the rural economy as much as their neighbors or wives who remain at home. Until they pass middle age, they can always return to South Africa if they are faced with financial need.

Overall then, the electoral participation factor shows a noticeable association in the rural areas with certain aspects of the respondents' economic situation and not a syncretistic or general social mobilization character. None of the specific economic factors, however, is very effective in terms of the proportion of variance they explain. More precise economic indicators of income or occupation might support interpretations of change in electoral activity which are related to social class or interest group mobilization.[26]

At the least, the above analysis casts serious doubt on the cumulative social mobilization model as far as its relevance to electoral participation within a country of Botswana's socio-economic and political circumstances. The social mobilization factor which showed a definite connection with awareness of the change in local government structures and moral support for such a change does not lead to behavioral change as far as the least intense forms of mass electoral activities, such as voting, attending meetings and being a member of a party. Factors which isolated particular aspects of rural economic involvement and which do not reflect a general social mobilization proved to be more effective as a basis for explanation. Indeed, migration to a developed economy, which in mobilization theory should reflect a whole melange of socio-economic influences leading to modernized political behavior, played a negative role particularly in the rural areas.

Intense Participation

This factor offers the clearest indication of socio-economic syncretism of any of the mass involvement dimensions being considered in this essay. It will be recalled that the three high loading variables for this factor on the varimax rotation were contacting the chief and councilors and concern about issues before the council. In inself, this dimension reflected an overlapping of participation in the traditional and modern political structures. In Table III, the two socio-economic factors with the highest relative connection are modern social mobilization (.26) and traditional social status (.18). Regardless of the subgroup examined, urban or rural, male or female, owners of more than 25 cattle or those who hold less, this dichotomous socio-economic influence pattern holds up, the most substantial manifestation being among rural females where the betas are .33 for modern social mobilization and .20 for traditional social status. Since these two socio-economic factors are orthogonal with each other, their correlations with intense participation indicate that persons active at this level of mass involvement tend to come from one of two different backgrounds: modern social mobilization or traditional social status. The syncretism evidenced is of two types: those with traditional status crossing over to participate in the modern system *and* the socially mobilized moving into the traditional system at least to the extent of making contact with the chief.

In direct contrast to electoral participation, the five economic factors have minimal connection with the intense participation factor. None of the subgroup betas are above .10 except for a few related to rural females. The rural females have a beta of .16 for the connection of rural economic involvement with intense participation, and those with 25 or less cattle have betas of -.14 for the association of labor migration to South Africa and private employment with the same dimension. The correlation of rural economic involvement with intense participation among rural females is reduced to .03 when owners of more than 25 cattle are removed. It would appear that females who are intensely involved in the modern market system as a result of either the sale of cattle or, when they do not have cattle, through the wages they earn in South Africa or by private employment in Botswana are more likely than those who are not so involved in the market to participate intensely in local politics. Outside of these relatively small female groups, however, economic involvement in and of itself does not seem to have much connection with intense participation. Traditional and modern social mobilization are much more important.

The beta weight pattern of the seven socio-economic factors differs substantially among the dependent political indexes examined thus far. Awareness of and moral support for the new council structure are definitely connected to social mobilization. Mass electoral behavior has almost no modern social mobilization basis but does reflect some impact of the intensity of rural economic involvement. In essence, these first three factors yield varying degrees of confirmation for the socio-economic mobilization hypothesis, the first two in terms of a general social mobilization effect and the latter in terms of involvement in the cash economy. Intense participation, on the other hand, supports the socio-economic syncretism hypothesis. Both traditional activists and those who have been stimulated to participate by the social mobilization process tend to be involved. In Botswana at least, the modernizers and those of traditional status do not participate in separate political structures in attempting to influence the authoritative allocation of values in society. Rather they become involved in both the new and old structures of government. The character of the relation between the two groups is not very explicit in the data under analysis, though it would appear from our examination of the moral support factor that the socially mobilized tend to be morally supportive of the new structure while those with traditional social status are rather evenly divided in terms of moral judgments. At the very least, we can say that the social mobilization process has added a new group to those active in local politics but that there still is a tendency for the royal clan members to be more active in political influence activities than the commoner population even in the new system. The syncretism is that of the meeting of two groups rather than of traditional and modern socio-economic influences combining to produce a new type of behavior on the part of individual citizens.

The consequences of this twofold basis for political activism are likely to depend on the way the activists are organized in a particular developing state. As we have already noted, Botswana political parties have from the very beginning been inclined to incorporate both traditional and modern elites within their organizations. They are thus able to make contact with the attentive public in both political systems. Such a synthesis may provide a context for minimizing the conflict between supporters of modern and traditional authority. In a country such as Lesotho where each of the two main parties have tended to organize supporters of only one of these bases of activism, the effect is likely to be a continual conflict over the legitimacy of political authority (Weisfelder, 1972: 134-139).

Traditional Participation

This dimension has very little association with the seven socio-economic factors when the sample as a whole is analyzed (Table III); however, separation of the urban and rural subgroups reveals definite support for the socio-economic mobilization hypothesis within the former. Table IV gives the beta weights derived from a regression analysis of the two groups. While almost 25% of the urban respondents' behavior is explained by the equation, that for the rural populace is less than 2%. The most important independent variable within the towns is modern social mobilization which has a negative coefficient of .41. The other two significant socio-economic factors are labor migration to South Africa and traditional social status, both of which are positively connected with traditional participation. Labor migration has almost the same effect within the rural sample. On the other hand, the impact of *both* the social mobilization and traditional status factors is limited to the urban areas with the former being negative and the latter positive—a decisive socio-economic mobilization pattern. The socially mobilized do not consider contact with chiefs and headmen to be any longer necessary in the urban context while those who have status within the traditional system are inclined to continue such relations.

Some recent studies of socio-economic mobilization have provided evidence that the urban context in itself has little effect on changing patterns of participation, (Inkeles, 1969: 1137-1138; Nie et al.,

1969: 364-368). With respect to the council participation factors considered above, this thesis generally applied—the most significant gap being the somewhat stronger connection of modern social mobilization with moral support for the council structure in the urban areas (.33) as compared with the countryside (.17). On the other hand, a clear socio-economic mobilization effect for traditional participation is *only* evident in the towns—both in terms of the negative association

TABLE IV

BETA WEIGHTS FOR THE URBAN AND RURAL SUBSAMPLES IN
REGRESSION EQUATION FOR TRADITIONAL PARTICIPATION

		Urban	Rural
1.	Modern Social Mobilization	-.41	.01
2.	Labor Migration to South Africa	.00	.03
3.	Labor Migration to South Africa (Spouse)	.16	.11
4.	Private Employment	.10	.00
5.	Rural Economic Involvement	.05	.07
6.	Self-employment	.02	.05
7.	Traditional Social Status	.17	.00
Multiple Correlation Coefficient		.49**	.14

** Significant at $\leq$ .001

of the social mobilization factor and the positive one for traditional status factor. The difference stems from at least several considerations. In part, it is due to the absence of a significant traditional structure in the urban context and the effective presence of such a structure in the rural areas. There are traditional authorities who claim some authority over both the towns surveyed, but for the average citizen the role of these authorities is almost completely symbolic. The colonial rulers effectively assumed almost all administrative powers even before the emergence of Tswana self-government. Also, the difference between the rural and urban areas with respect to traditional participation is explained by the fact that those who have experienced less social mobilization are much more likely to be temporary residents of the towns and thus inclined to return to the countryside where traditional authorities clearly retain much political power. They are, thus, more likely than the rest of the urban population to have both the opportunity and reason to become involved in the traditional system.

The beta weight pattern for this factor combined with those preceding it provides a basis for several generalizations about the character of the political change process which is occurring at the mass level in Botswana. First, those who are mobilized in the urban environment may cease participation in the traditional system but they do not necessarily replace it with what might be considered a comparable form of participation in the council system; namely, taking part in electoral activities. Indeed, the correlation between the electoral factor and modern social mobilization is only .12 in the urban areas. It may be that while the traditional system has been rejected, a state of anomie exists among many affected by social mobilization as far as the institutional structure which is to serve as their means of influence in the new environment. Second, within the rural areas, the socially mobilized do not show any trend with respect to both the traditional or electoral mass participation surveyed in this study. They are not inclined to withdraw from the former or participate in the latter, even though they do show some sympathy for the council in moral terms. They may well judge the traditional authorities as still too potent in power terms to risk open opposition.

The five traditional participation items were included in the questionnaire expressly to examine the extent to which social mobilization affects involvement in the traditional system. In many analyses, it has been assumed that increasing involvement with modern political structures is accompanied by a withdrawal from traditional ones. That there has been such a withdrawal has not actually been tested. The preceding analysis emphasizes the need to explore the impact of social mobilization on traditional political behavior. In this instance, the social mobilization which makes people aware and supportive of the new council structures does not bring a decline of involvement in traditional politics in the rural areas even when such an effect is occurring in substantial proportions in the new towns. Clearly, analysis of political change requires increased precision as to both dimensions of change being considered and the context in which it is transpiring.

VII. CONCLUSION

The above analysis has concerned the dimensional character of citizen political involvement in the traditional and modern local government structures of Botswana and the extent to which this involvement reflects the social mobilization and syncretistic models of change. Principal components analysis established the most general groupings of the political involvement variables related to the two political systems. Moral support for the new council structure was associated with awareness of legal changes brought by the new system, some forms of participation in it, and a hesitation to accept commands any longer from the traditional political authorities. This dimension clearly reflected substantial mobilization of various forms of political perception and action, in terms of both movement toward the modern system and away from the older one. A less intense but significant polarization was manifested by the third principal component in which several of the responses concerning attachment to the local Tswana community were negatively associated with voting in council elections and party membership.

The second principal component included almost all of the traditional and modern participation items in positive association with each other. In this regard, a definite syncretistic pattern was established. While awareness of the new council structures and support for these structures showed some mobilization effect, it would appear that the new forms of participation associated with these structures are also influenced by existing Tswana modes of politics as well.

With the varimax analysis, our Tswana respondents reflected much less mobilization and syncretism. Such a retrenchment is not surprising in that this form of factor analysis highlights only the most substantial forms of association in a data matrix. Four of the originally postulated minimal dimensions of social mobilization emerged: awareness of the legal change to elected councils, moral support for the change, mass participation in council structures, and traditional participation. In addition, the original set of political cohesion items were divided into two groups, one reflecting psychic mobility and the other parochialism. The varimax analysis identified only one substantial form of syncretism among the involvement variables, that of intense participation in both the traditional and modern political systems.

The exploration of the relation of a selected set of socio-economic variables with political involvement utilized the varimax factor dimensions mentioned in the preceding paragraph. The socio-economic variables were also grouped into factor dimensions by a similar approach. The variation in the degree of association between specific socio-economic dimensions, on the one hand, and the various political factors, on the other, was substantial. A general socio-economic mobilization dimension had a very dramatic connection with the legal awareness dimension and a somewhat moderate one with moral approval of the new structure of local government. In the urban areas, socio-economic mobilization also showed an impact on withdrawal from traditional political activities. Mass political activities, i.e., those associated very directly with elections, had a strong relationship in the rural areas with a series of factors reflecting intense involvement in the market economy, while socio-economic mobilization showed little effect. The intense participation factor was the only one which showed a pronounced syncretistic connection with socio-economic variables, specifically the social mobilization and the traditional status factors.

Two aspects of the relationship between the socio-economic and the political factors should be noted. First, the pattern of association varied. Most important for this study, socio-economic mobilization had a substantial positive association with awareness of political change, and a very strong negative connection with traditional participation in the urban context. With the other political dimensions, social mobilization had a much less significant impact. In short, there is good reason to believe that the impact of socio-economic change depends on the political dimensions being considered. Second, in the study of political change in dimensional terms, it would appear that the more specific dimensions produced by varimax should be utilized rather than the general dimensions of involvement which emerged from principal components analysis. For instance, the latter created one component with regard to participation which was divided into three factors by varimax. Each of these three factors had a very different relation with the seven socio-economic dimensions used in this study. In essence, there is good reason to believe that the general factor dimensions of principal components analysis may combine forms of activity which are uniquely affected by socio-economic change.

Although a number of different dimensions of political involvement exist within Botswana politics, the foregoing analysis does provide a basis for making generalizations about citizen involvement as a whole in this African country. The more passive forms of mass politics show the most dramatic evidence of a mobilization process. In particular, the dimensions of awareness of legal change and support for the new political structure covary with each other as well as being affected by the general factor of socio-economic modernization. The most intense forms of involvement, on the other hand, appear most likely to manifest a syncretistic pattern. Thus, the varimax rotation produced a participation factor which included contact activity with both the chief and the local councilors and evidence of concern about local political issues. This activity is also syncretistic with respect to its socio-economic basis in that persons of traditional status and those affected by modernization are more likely than the rest of the population to participate at this higher level of intensity.

For the moderate intensity forms of involvement such as voting and attending political meetings, both mobilization and syncretism are manifested to some extent. The electoral activities factor in the varimax analysis indicates a mobilization of low intensity participation within the council system. Its lack of connection in a positive sense with the items concerning moral support establishes that the mobilization is not very extensive. A minimal amount of syncretism also exists among the participation items in that all but one have significant loadings on the second principal component.

It is very possible that these moderate intensity forms of involvement are better explained as a function of factors analagous to those operating in more developed polities; specifically, group interest and organization, social class and family background. Nie, Powell, and Prewitt (1969) examine this type of involvement in their study of the Almond-Verba five nation data, though they do include some high intensity items in their general participation index. They conclude that the expansion of group membership and social class are two central factors affecting the expansion of citizen participation. In the present analysis of Botswana, the limited but quite clearly important connection of various forms of intense rural market activity with the electoral participation factor shows evidence of a group interest factor operating. It is possible that if such groups become organized as is likely to be the case with more economic development, a group membership effect similar to that identified by Nie et al. will become operative.

The extent to which these propositions concerning citizen politics in Botswana are relevant to other developing countries very much depends on the character of a given socio-economic and political context. Even within Botswana we have established that considerable variations may occur because of differences in community structure. The most incisive evidence in this regard concerned traditional participation. In the rural areas, the social mobilization factor exercised very little influence in drawing people away from traditional political activities; however, in the new towns, it was associated with a very marked withdrawal. A number of other system influences on variations in the pattern of mobilization and syncretism in citizen politics were suggested including those related to the degree of party organization, economic development and modern versus traditional elite conflict.

Politics in a society are best understood from a number of perspectives. In Africa, analysis has tended to concentrate on the various elite strata, the traditional authorities, colonial rulers, nationalist leaders, the emergent bourgeoisie, civil servants, and students. Within political science, very few scholars have examined the character of mass political involvement in any great detail. This paper offers one approach for achieving an understanding of citizen politics. In particular, we have explored the utility of a multidimensional perspective of political involvement and a theory concerning the relevance of mobilization and syncretism in explaining various dimensions. The utility of both for developing countries other than Botswana requires similar projects in a number of different environments. Until such research is undertaken, our understanding of politics at the individual level must be limited largely to interpretations provided by indigenous elites and the speculations generated by scholars studying these elites. In a very real sense, Africanist political science has not penetrated African societies much more than the European colonial rulers who drew their perspective of the political order from persons who were or pretended to be the elites in a given area. Needless to say, such research is bound to be threatening to both Africans and non-Africans in that the results may run counter to deeply ingrained myths.

NOTES

1. Zolberg (1966) provides a good summary of the type of research which was done up to the mid-sixties on both institution building and the character of the elite election process. The lack of analysis of mass political involvement is particularly serious in rural areas of Africa; in this regard see A. Magid (1969: 92). Two notable recent examinations of citizen behavior are both based on largely urban samples: Robert Melson (1971), Alex Inkeles (1969).

2. Botswana was named Bechuanaland by the British during the colonial period. Most of the people in this country are of the "Tswana" culture. They are called "Batswana" as a group, and one person is referred to as a "Motswana."

3. The final tabulations on the 1966 local government elections are reported in the *Bechuanaland Daily News,* June 15, 1966, pp. 1-2; the 1969 results in *Report on the General Elections 1969* (Gaberone, Botswana: Government Printer, n.d.), pp. 58-84. A brief discussion of the issues in the 1969 election is provided by A.J. Macartney (1969). For data on the 1965 and 1969 Parliamentary elections, see the supplement to *Bechuanaland Daily News,* March 1, 1965, pp. 1-3; and *Report on the General Elections 1969*, pp. 49-57.

4. The Botswana People's Party (BPP) won a majority in the Francistown and North

East councils in both 1966 and 1969. It also collected over 40% of the elected seats in the Kgatleng District. The Botswana National Front (BNF) gained 50% of the seats in 1969 in the towns of Gaberone and Lobatse. The BNF also was over 40% in Ngwaketse District in 1969. The Botswana Independence Party obtained over 40% of the seats in the North West in 1969 and in combination with the BPP, it did the same in 1966.

5. Recent discussions of the concept of modernization have emphasized the need for greater rigor in the definition of the concept. Three articles were particularly helpful for this paper: Armer and Schnaiberg (1972), Charlick (1973), and Portes (1973).

6. The classic statements of this model are provided by Lerner (1958) and Deutsch (1961). Representative of research done in Africa from this perspective are Apter (1963, 1965), Busia (1968), Coleman and Rosberg (1964), Hodgkin (1961), Morgenthau (1964).

7. Deutsch (1961), and Lerner (1958).

8. Similar analyses are to be found relating to other areas of the world as well; for instance, Gusfield (1967) draws on his experience in India to develop a syncretistic analysis.

9. See also on syncretistic models in the study of African politics, Gluckman (1970), Epstein (1958), Uchendu (1970), Plotnicov (1970).

10. Nie, Powell, and Prewitt (1969) are concerned with the problem of dimensionality in constructing their political participation index to the extent that they require all items included to have a loading of $\geq$ .50 for the first factor of an unrotated principal components matrix. It is not clear how many items were in the original correlation matrix or why items included for the United States were not exactly the same as those used in the other four countries. As will be pointed out, the principal components approach tends to maximize the range of items included in a dimension. As a consequence, it reduces markedly the possibility of exploring differential impacts of socio-economic change on specific types of political behavior.

Inkeles (1969) also recognizes the dimensional character of citizen involvement but chooses to combine his subscales into one overall scale which he terms "participant citizenship." In five of the six countries Inkeles studies, this index does not meet the Nie, Powell and Prewitt criterion of dimensionality, namely a loading of $\geq$ .50 on the first unrotated principal component for variables used in its composition. Specifically, Argentina has two of the five subscales below this level (.35 for allegiance and .49 for rationality); Nigeria one (.35 for rationality); Chile one (.25 for allegiance); Israel two (.49 for allegiance and .48 for rationality); and East Pakistan one (.36 for rationality). Each subscale was composed of three to seven questions that may also have not represented a single dimension according to the Nie, Powell and Prewitt criterion; however, no test was possible because the Inkeles article does not contain the data required.

11. The term "involvement" as used in this study is defined to include any type of citizen association with politics, whether perceptual or actual behavioral. Sometimes, (e.g., Inkeles, 1969), the word "participation" is used in a broad sense which includes both these forms of involvement. In this paper, participation refers to "action" types of political behavior. See Weiner (1971: 164) and Hayward (1973: 354) for recent use of this more limited definition.

12. The communal character of politics in traditional societies has long been emphasized in the social sciences. On the character of nineteenth and early twentieth century sociological thought on community, see Nisbet (1966). Recent studies emphasizing the importance of a sense of community in the traditional political system are Lerner (1958), Pye (1962), Huntington (1968).

13. Interviews with Agricultural Department officials in charge of extension work.

14. The primary objective of this section is reduction of the participation data to its

essential dimensions. This objective necessitates an examination of all the variance in the original data and not just that variance which the items have in common. As a consequence, unities were inserted in the principal diagonal of the correlation matrix rather than a communality estimate. For a particularly clear statement of the problem of entries in the principal diagnoal and the rationale for the procedure employed in this paper, see Vincent (1971). The factor analysis reported in this essay was performed with the use of the SOUPAC programs developed by the Statistical Consultants of the Department of Computer Science, University of Illinois (Urbana Campus).

15. Several oblique rotations were also performed on the principal components factor matrix. The factor loading patterns did not differ substantially from that of the orthogonal. In an oblimax solution, five of the combinations among the seven reference vectors had a correlation of .2 or more, and in a binormamin solution, three combinations reached a similar extent of association.

16. For instance, it was simply not realistic to ask a question soliciting the respondent's monetary income because of the distortion and resistance which such a question encountered.

17. Varimax was used for the creation of factor scores because it highlights dimensions based on variables which are highly intercorrelated, and concomitantly produces a set of factors which are not correlated with each other. The former advantage minimizes the confusion as to what a particular factor score means, and the latter insures that there is no overlap between the various factor scores in terms of dimensions measured.

18. Factor VII also reflects a greater tendency among those who load high on this dimension to be connected with Christianity presently or in the past. This should not distort the traditional status character of this factor in that, as was mentioned above, the Tswana elite has shown since the turn of the century a strong inclination to include Christianity within the traditional social structure.

19. The analysis in this section follows the general approach suggested by Vincent (1971) for the use of factor scores in multiple regression analysis. The formula for the calculation of factor scores is $F = ZR^{-1}A$, where F is a matrix of factor scores, Z is a matrix of standard scores for the original variables, R is the matrix of intercorrelation among the original variables, and A is the factor structure matrix. The matrix program of SOUPAC was used for these calculations.

20. I formulated these definitions with the assistance of Robert Charlick.

21. For this section of the analysis, the sample size was reduced to 553 respondents who had no missing data in the two original data matrices. Had mean values been used where missing data existed, the effect would have been to drive the correlations down somewhat. Since the sample contained over a thousand respondents, it was feasible to select out those having missing data and still retain an adequate number of respondents. A check of the frequency distribution for this reduced sample revealed no substantial change except for a slight gain in the portion of those with over three years of education and those with regular media contact. A factor analysis of the original political involvement and socio-economic data matrices was also undertaken for the reduced sample. The same factors emerged with verv little difference in the loadings.

Since the sample has been reduced by those respondents having missing data, the correlation coefficients are not exactly the same as the beta weights. Such a correspondence of the correlation coefficients and beta weights only occurs for two sets of factors if all the cases in the original data matrix are used. Where the betas are more than .02 away from the correlation coefficients, the latter are also given in parentheses in Table III.

22. The sizes of the subsamples used in the subsequent analysis are as follows: urban (127), rural (426), rural with 25 or less cattle (337), rural female (188), rural female with 25 or less cattle (136), rural male (238), rural male with 25 or less cattle (201).

23. For data indicating Botswana's relative poverty within Africa, see D.G. Morrison, R.C. Mitchell, J.N. Paden and H.M. Stevenson (1972: 51). Botswana ranks in the ninth decile among 32 African countries in a table delineating per capita GNP in 1968.

24. See also S.M. Lipset (1960: 29-63).

25. In Morrison et al. (1972: 98), Botswana ranks in the tenth decile in a table specifying the number of years from the establishment of the first political party in a country through 1970.

26. Also supporting the impact of organization membership on citizen involvement in Botswana is a recent paper by Vengroff (1972).

APPENDIX I: INTERVIEW CONTEXT AND SAMPLE CHARACTER

The interviews were conducted in August and early September since these months are the best times of the year to draw a random and large rural sample in Botswana. After the harvest season is over in July, most of the rural population comes together in a limited number of villages and towns. Some of the latter contain as much as thirty or forty thousand people. Within each village and town, fairly clear principles operate to determine the location of the traditional wards which constitute the essential political substructure of every traditional rural political community. Thus, by using the wards as units to be sampled (approximately ten persons were drawn from each ward), it was possible to establish a basis for an area sample that insured a variety of respondents in terms of traditional spatial living patterns. In addition, because the population was concentrated in a limited number of residential areas during the interviewing period, i.e., August and September, a good portion of the rural populace in Southern Botswana could be sampled with the financial resources available for the project.

In the cities, the sample was drawn from the populace living in the wage-earning and lower-salary income areas. The population not sampled is essentially middle class, namely those working in positions previously held primarily by Europeans or those owning relatively prosperous business enterprises by Tswana standards. In the lexicon of Southern Africa, we sampled the "townships." The middle class Batswana of the cities were excluded because of their very small number in comparison to the total population and because this study was concerned with the mass of the populace rather than what is essentially the ruling elite of this newly independent African state.

Every effort was made to facilitate the response to the questionnaire within the medium of the Tswana culture. The six interviewers all spoke Setswana as their first language. The questions used in the survey were translated into Setswana by a teacher of the language and then checked for meaning by having a generally recognized expert in Setswana translation transpose the questions back into English. The author, who has a partial knowledge of Setswana, explored extensively the meaning of particular political concepts which were used in some of the questions. Because it is not customary for people of the opposite sex to discuss economic and political matters, the interview staff only contacted those of their own sex. Finally, it is not considered proper for outsiders to make contact with people in a village without first asking the consent of the local chief or headman. Therefore, a series of interviews was never begun in an area without first approaching the local chief or headman for his approval. In every case, the traditional authorities were quite willing to grant approval.

Since the sample is stratified to assure a minimum number from various social groups, the frequency distribution in socio-economic terms differs somewhat from that of the population for the interviewing area. In the table below, the frequency distributions for the sample on a number of variables are compared with those calculated for the population on the basis of the 1964 Census and the 1968-69 Agricultural Survey. It will be observed that the sample which is being used in this study somewhat exceeds the general population distribution in the following categories: urbanization, males, those under 30 and over 59 years of age, the more educated, Bamalete and Batlokwa, and wage earners. The proportion of holders of 25 or less cattle is also above the sample distributions which the Agricultural Department obtained in its most recent survey of the five tribal areas examined in this study. In part, this outcome is due to the over-representation of two groups with few cattle, namely the urban residents and the Bamalete. Also, since rural tax rates are based on herd size, some interviewees may have feared that a correct answer might lead to an increase in their assessments. To minimize any effect of an undervaluing of cattle holdings, this variable was dichotomized as follows: holders of more than 25 cattle and those with 25 or less. Even with this modification, it is likely that cattle holding may be a somewhat more significant variable than indicated by correlation coefficients.

APPENDIX I (cont.)

SAMPLE AND POPULATION DISTRIBUTIONS FOR
SOME SOCIO-ECONOMIC VARIABLES

VARIABLE	SAMPLE	POPULATION
Rural	33%	44%
Tribal Capitals	43%	41%
Urban (a)	25%	15%
SEX (b)		
Female	45%	52%
Male	54%	48%
AGE (b)		
20-29 Years	25%	30%
30-39 Years	26%	23%
40-49 Years	20%	17%
50-59 Years	14%	13%
60-69 Years	11%	9%
70 and Over	3%	7%
Omitted	2%	.7%
EDUCATION (b)		
No Education	39%	70%
Standard I-III	20%	20%
Standard IV-VI	20%	6%
Standard VII-Form II of J.C.	13%	1%
J.C. and Above	6%	1%
Omitted	1%	2%
CATTLE HOLDING (c)		
No Cattle	47%	23%
1-25 Cattle	38%	48%
26-50 Cattle	9%	17%
51-100 Cattle	3%	8%
Over 100 Cattle	2%	4%
Omitted	1%	

-Continued-

APPENDIX I (cont.)

VARIABLE	SAMPLE	POPULATION
ETHNIC MEMBERSHIP (d)		
Bakgatla	22%	28%
Bakwena	17%	32%
Bamalete	12%	7%
BaNgwaketse	20%	30%
Batlokwa	7%	2%
Other	20%	
WAGE EARNERS (e)		
Wage Earners	46%	43%
Non-Wage Earners	53%	57%
Omitted	1%	

((The populations are calculated on the basis of data available in Report on the Census of the Bechuanaland Protectorate 1964; (Mafeking, n.d.), and The 1963/69 Agricultural Survey (Gaberone, 1970).))

(a) Gaberone, the new capital of Botswana, was sampled but had only a small populace at the time of the 1964 census. Therefore, I have used estimates of the present population.

(b) The population distributions do not include the urban areas.

(c) The cattle frequency for the total population is only for Ngwaketse, Kweneng, Kgatleng and Tlokweng. Bamalete and the urban areas have much less cattle holdings. Therefore, the population from which the sample is drawn is not as far off the sample as it appears.

(d) Population frequencies are the total population of the five tribal areas and are not adjusted for strangers living in each of the areas, except Bakgatla living in Ngwaketse and Kweneng.

(e) The population distribution of wage earners is a very rough estimate. It assumes that 8% are employed in non-agricultural occupations within Botswana in the five tribal areas; that over 50% of the urban population is earning wages; that the 18% of the rural population in the five areas earns some wages from farm labor in Botswana; and that 8% of the population has worked in South Africa within the past year. These estimates are derived from the Agricultural Survey.

APPENDIX II

VARIMAX FACTORS OF THE TWENTY-ONE SOCIO-ECONOMIC INDICATORS*

	I	II	III	IV	V	VI	VII	COMMUNALITIES
1. Residence: Rural/Urban	.32						-.38	.37
2. Sex: Female/Male			-.38	.66				.68
3. Age	-.44			.36			.37	.52
4. Source of food: market/subsistence		.74						.53
5. Religion: non-Christian/Christian	.37					.36		.48
6. Education: number of years	.77						.42	.70
7. Newspaper reading: never to daily	.80							.67
8. Radio listening: never to daily	.75			-.30				.58
9. Family cultivates fields: no/yes		.75						.63
10. Family raises cattle: no/yes		.72						.59
11. Family member works in government: no/yes	.50				-.59	-.33		.78
12. Family member works in private employment: no/yes					.89			.87
13. Family member self-employed (non-agriculture):no/yes						.90		.84
14. Labor migrant in South Africa: no/yes				.82				.71
15. Number of years in South Africa				.82				.71
16. Spouse a labor migrant in South Africa: no/yes			.88					.79
17. Number of years for spouse's migration			.86					.74
18. Number of cattle owned: 25 or less/more than 25	.31	.65						.53
19. Status in traditional society: commoner/royal							.74	.57
20. Wage earner: no/yes	.54	-.34						.52
21. Spouse wage earner: no/yes			.71					.59
Percentage of Total Variance Explained by the Factors	21.9	17.8	16.9	15.8	10.0	8.8	8.6	

*Respondents with missing data on any pair of variables were excluded from the calculation of the correlation coefficient for the two variables. Unities were used in the diagonal of the correlation matrix. The cutoff point for the determination of principal components was an eigenvalue of 1. The principal components analysis explained 64% of the total variance in the original data matrix. All associations with the factors $\geq$ .30 are reported.

REFERENCES

APTER, D.E. (1963) Ghana in Transition. New York: Athenaeum.
———(1965) The Politics of Modernization. Chicago: Univ. of Chicago Press.
ARMER, M. and A. SCHNAIBERG (1972) "Measuring individual modernity." American Sociological Rev. 37 (June).
ARMER, M. and R. YOUTZ (1971) "Formal education and individual modernity in an African society." American Journal of Sociology 76 (January).
BUSIA, K.A. (1968) The Position of the Chief in the Modern Political System of Ashanti. London: Frank Cass & Co.
CHARLICK, R. (1973) "What leads to modernization?—a comment on research trends." Journal of Modern African Studies XI (March).
COLEMAN, J.S. and C.G. ROSBERG, Jr., (1964) [eds.] Political Parties and National Integration in Tropical Africa. Berkeley and Los Angeles: Univ. of California Press.
DEUTSCH, K. (1961) "Social mobilization and political development." American Political Science Rev. LV (September).
EPSTEIN, A.L. (1958) Politics in an Urban African Community. Manchester: Manchester Univ. Press.
GLUCKMAN, M. (1970) "Tribalism in modern British Central Africa." in I.L. Markovitz (ed.) African Politics and Society. New York: Free Press.
GOEL, M.L. (1970) "The relevance of education for political participation in a developing society." Comparative Political Studies 3 (October).
GUSFIELD, J.R. (1967) "Tradition and modernity: misplaced polarities in the study of change." American Journal of Sociology 72 (January).
HAYWARD, F.M. (1973) "Political participation and its role in development: some observations drawn from the African context." Journal of Developing Areas 7 (July).
HODGKIN, T. (1961) African Political Parties. Baltimore: Penguin Books.
HOLM, J.D. (1972) "Rural development in Botswana: three basic political trends." Rural Africana 18 (Fall).
HUNTINGTON, S.P. (1968) Political Order in Changing Societies. New Haven: Yale Univ. Press.
INKELES, A. (1969) "Participant citizenship in six developing countries." American Political Science Rev. LXIII (December).
KOMA, K. (n.d.) Botswana National Front Pamphlet No. 1. Gaberone.
LERNER, D. (1958) The Passing of Traditional Society. New York: Free Press.
LIPSET, S.M. (1960) Political Man: The Social Basis of Politics. Garden City, New York: Doubleday & Company.
MAGID, A. (1969) "Political Science priorities in local African research," in N. Miller (ed.) Research in Rural Africa. Lansing: African Studies Center of Michigan State University.
McCRONE, D.J. and C.F. CNUDDE (1967) "Towards a communications theory of democratic political development: a causal model." American Political Science Rev. LXI (March).
MELSON, R. (1971) "Ideology and inconsistence: the 'cross-pressured' Nigerian worker." American Political Science Rev. LXV (March).
MILLER, N. (1966) "The political survival of traditional leadership." Journal of Modern African Studies 6 (August).
MORRISON, D.G., R.C. MITCHELL, J.N. PADEN and H.M. STEVENSON (1972) Black Africa: A Comparative Handbook. New York: Free Press.

MORGAN, N. and J.A. SONQUIST (1963) "Problems in the analysis of survey data, and a proposal." Journal of the American Statistical Association 58 (June).

MORGENTHAU, R.S. (1964) Political Parties in French-Speaking Africa. Oxford: The Clarendon Press.

NEEDLER, M.C. (1968) "Political participation and socioeconomic development: the case of Latin America." American Political Science Rev. LXII (September).

NIE, N.H., G.B. POWELL, Jr., and K. PREWITT (1969) "Social structure and political participation: development relationships, part 1." American Political Science Rev. LXIII (June).

NISBET, R.A. (1966) The Sociological Tradition. New York: Basic Books.

PLOTNICOV, L. (1970) "Rural-urban communications in contemporary Nigeria: the persistence of traditional social institutions." Journal of Asian and African Studies V (January and April).

PORTES, A. (1973) "The factorial structure of modernity: empirical replications and a critique." American Journal of Sociology 79 (July).

PYE, L.W. (1962) Politics, Personality, and Nation Building: Burma's Search for Identity. New Haven: Yale Univ. Press.

RUMMEL, R.J. (1970) Applied Factor Analysis. Evanston: Northwestern Univ. Press.

SCHAPERA, I. (1970) A Handbook of Tswana Law and Custom. London: Frank Cass & Co.

———(1952) The Ethnic Composition of the Tswana Tribes. London: London School of Economics.

SILLERY, A. (1952) The Bechuanaland Protectorate. London: Oxford Univ. Press.

SKINNER, E.P. (1960) "Labor migration and its relationship to socio-cultural change in Mossi society." Africa XXX (no. 2).

UCHENDU, V.D. (1970) "The passing of tribal man: a West African experience." Journal of Asian and African Studies V (January and April).

VENGROFF, R. (1972) "Education and political development in Botswana: an exploratory study." A paper prepared for delivery at the 1972 annual meetings of the African Studies Association, Philadelphia, Pennsylvania, November 8-11.

VERBA S., N.H. NIE and J. KIM (1971) The Modes of Democratic Participation: A Cross-National Comparison, Beverly Hills: Sage Publications.

VERBA, S., N.H. NIE, A. BARBIC, G. IRWIN, H. MOLLEMAN, and G. SHABAD (1973) "The modes of participation: continuities in research." Comparative Political Studies 6 (July).

VINCENT, J.E. (1971) Factor Analysis in International Relations. Gainsville: Univ. of Florida Press.

WALLERSTEIN, I. (1961) Africa: The Politics of Independence. New York: Vintage Books.

WEINER, M. (1971) "Political participation: crisis of the political process." in L. Binder, J.S. Coleman, J. LaPalombara, L.W. Pye, S. Verba, and M. Weiner: Crises and Sequences in Political Development. Princeton: Princeton Univ. Press.

WEISFELDER, R.F. (1972) "Lesotho" in C.P. Potholm and R. Dale (eds.) Southern Africa in Perspective. New York: Free Press.

WHITAKER, S. (1970) The Politics of Tradition, Continuity and Change in Northern Nigeria: 1946-1966. Princeton: Princeton Univ. Press.

ZOLBERG, A.R. (1966) Creating Political Order: The Party States of West Africa. Chicago: Rand McNally & Co.

JOHN D. HOLM is Associate Professor of Political Science at Cleveland State University. His primary research interest is the study of political change as viewed from various socio-political perspectives using empirical techniques. He has undertaken field work in Africa and has published essays on Botswana, Ghana, and Lesotho. Currently, he is involved in research projects concerned with the authority perceptions of various Tswana elite groups, the transformation of public opinion in the United States in regard to Watergate-generated issues, and the potential for secondary analysis of a number of quantitative data sets related to political change in Africa.